W9-ARL-980

SUCCESSFUL
HOME GREENHOUSES

7.

SUCCESSFUL HOME GREENHOUSES

William Scheller

Structures Publishing Company
Farmington, Michigan 1977

Copyright © 1977 Structures Publishing Co.
Farmington, Michigan

All rights reserved, including those of translation. This book, or parts thereof, may not be reproduced in any form without permission of the copyright owner. Neither the author, nor the publisher, by publication of data in this book, ensure to anyone the use of such data against liability of any kind, including infringement of any patent. Publication of data in this book does not constitute a recommendation of any patent or proprietary right that may be involved.

Manufactured in the United States of America

Editor: Shirley M. Horowitz

Production Editor: Dixie Clark

Cover photo courtesy of Lord & Burnham

Current printing (last digit)
10 9 8 7 6 5 4 3 2 1

Structures Publishing Co.
Box 423, Farmington, Mich. 48024

Library of Congress Cataloging in Publication Data

Scheller, William.
    Successful home greenhouses.

    Includes index.
    1. Greenhouses—Design and construction. I. Title.
SB416.S33   690'.8'9   76-51747
ISBN 0-912336-40-4
ISBN 0-912336-41-2 pbk.

CONTENTS

INTRODUCTION

No one in America today can be unaware of the tremendous revival of interest in houseplants. At the same time, a passion for outdoor gardening has united city, suburban, and rural dwellers alike. What could be more natural than an increasing desire to bring these two leisure activities together—and where else but under the greenhouse roof?

Greenhouses are no longer a plaything of the elite. They are a common sight today, whether standing freely, attached to a home, perched on a roof, or clinging to an apartment window. Manufacturers of prefabricated kits have brought the size and cost of greenhouses within the average person's reach, and the do-it-yourselfer can select from a wide variety of plans for backyard installations. There is a greenhouse for every gardener.

This book has been written for all prospective greenhouse gardeners. It outlines the fundamentals of greenhouse construction in each style and size category, and takes into consideration varying requirements for different areas of the country as well as those arising from particular home designs and grounds layout.

Beginning with a discussion of the possibilities and advantages of a home greenhouse for everyone from the flower enthusiast to the vegetable gardener, the book describes the many shapes and styles of greenhouse, outlines their construction features, and familiarizes the reader with the materials available for the kit builder or complete do-it-yourselfer. Also included are chapters on heating and environmental control, and a look at the most useful fixtures and tools for making greenhouse gardening easy and rewarding. Finally, there are guides to soil preparation, plant selection, and individual plant location within the greenhouse, and recommended sources of kits, plans, and technical information.

Chapter 1 ADVANTAGES OF A HOME GREENHOUSE

There are many thousands of people gardening today who once thought the vegetable patch something quaint and rural, and cultivation of exotic flowers a pastime for the leisured few. No doubt many of these gardeners still harbor a similar view toward greenhouses—they may feel that glassed-in gardening is the province either of commercial growers, or of gentlemen retired to their estates.

It just isn't so.

A drive through the countryside, suburbs, or even built-up areas will show that greenhouses, while perhaps not gaining on garages, are certainly within the reach of people of moderate means who like to grow things. These people have realized that greenhouses truly broaden their gardening horizons. Neither size nor cost need be an object. There are greenhouse arrangements that take up no more room than a small porch or patio—or even a windowbox. In cities, greenhouses are beginning to appear perched atop flat roofs, or attached to the roofs of projecting lower stories.

The greenhouse is the place where the houseplant enthusiast and the outdoor gardener meet. Those devoted to indoor flowers and greenery know that many plant varieties require an environment more strictly regulated than that found in the average home. It is often not possible to adjust the temperature or humidity of the human environment to a level suitable to the fussier plant varieties. Sunlight, too, is often a problem, as anyone knows whose houseplants like to migrate from one window to another at different times of day. The greenhouse offers a climate capable of more precise regulation, and in which there is ample sunlight. Even plants that do well

This aluminum leanto greenhouse fits in perfectly with suburban living. Not only is it compatible with the home, but it takes up surprisingly little backyard space. (Courtesy Aluminum Greenhouses, Inc.)

Gardener working with plants in greenhouse.

These seedlings are growing in a separate propagating bed within the greenhouse. The plastic canopy overhead, along with a soil heating cable below, provides the extra warmth needed by certain plants early in their development.

in homes will do better in greenhouses, and new cuttings may be started there under optimum conditions. Plant lovers who have always purchased already-started specimens can begin to start many of the familiar varieties from seed. Begonia and coleus are two of the popular indoor species that germinate well in greenhouse seed flats.

Cacti, with their preference for a warm, arid environment and well-drained, sandy soil, can easily be pampered in the greenhouse. If the cultivation of these or any other variety requiring special conditions is to be combined in the home greenhouse with plants having different requirements, the gardener will find that his structure may easily be partitioned. Many companies supplying prefabricated greenhouses offer such partitions, and make allowance for possible future expansion in their basic designs.

STRETCHING THE GROWING SEASON

The outdoor gardener must be constantly concerned with growing conditions; he must deal with variations even more unpredictable than those faced by houseplant enthusiasts. In many parts of North America, the growing season is simply too short to allow cultivation of some beautiful ornamentals, such as snapdragons, forget-me-nots, petunias, and carnations. Even in places where warm weather arrives sufficiently early, the gardener will be pleased to be able to set out plants in full flower when they would normally be barely getting started. The greenhouse cuts winter down to size. It allows the gardener to give his seedlings a headstart before the last frost of spring, and it lets him cultivate warm-weather varieties on into late fall and winter. Less winter-hardy plants may be taken indoors during the cold season, eliminating the need for annual replacement.

Vegetables too

The ability to "get the jump" on spring is, of course, a boon to the vegetable gardener. Crops usually limited to southern areas, such as eggplant, pepper, okra, and bush lima beans, can be started as early as desired, and transplanted outdoors when spring is finally under way. Favorite compact-growing crops can be kept under glass throughout the year. The thought of fresh strawberries, asparagus, salad greens, and tomatoes on the table in

Not even the coldest weather need interfere with greenhouse gardening enjoyment. (Courtesy Lord & Burnham)

January is almost justification enough for a home greenhouse.

But guests' exclamations of "Where did you get those strawberries?" or the ability to snip a fresh corsage on New Year's Eve, are but a small part of the pleasures of greenhouse ownership. The real joy of it lies in knowing that there is always a corner of your home or garden that is pleasant, colorful, and full of live and growing things.

GREENHOUSES WITHIN REACH OF NEARLY ALL HOMEOWNERS

Virtually every hobby or avocation may be pursued on a scale adapted to the hobbyist's personal desires and financial capability. The fisherman can enjoy himself going after perch with a light spinning rod in a rented rowboat, or, if his resources allow, he can fight blue marlin from a chartered yacht in the Caribbean. The same is true of the greenhouse gardener. The extensiveness of his glassed-in domain depends upon his time, ability, and money. But the degree of his enjoyment is in no way connected to such factors as size or cost—it's directly related to his *enthusiasm*. Here we will focus upon low and moderate-cost structures, both prefabricated and built "from scratch," that will give free play to that enthusiasm.

Factors influencing cost

CONSTRUCTION   It would be entirely possible to build a rudimentary greenhouse for under $100, excluding a heating device. Such a structure would make use of locally available lumber—probably spruce or fir two-by-fours—and a flexible sheeting of polyurethane or vinyl. As we'll see in a later chapter, these inexpensive materials have their place in greenhouse design. But the light softwood frame and flexible covering are best suited for use in extremely mild climates, or as temporary units. So, while this least elaborate of greenhouse designs is inexpensive indeed, its uses are limited and its probable life-span short; thus, its price may be misleading.

The prospective builder interested in a solid, maintenance-free structure at a minimum expenditure had best look into the array of prefabricated models available in the $200 to $1,000 range or if the gardener has a modicum of manual skill, into plans for similar greenhouses incorporating many of the same reliable materials —redwood or aluminum for the frame; glass, fiberglass, or one of the stronger flexible plastics for the lights (window area).

Vegetables growing in greenhouse.

The question of whether to build a foundation— and if so, what kind to build—will largely depend upon climate. The necessity of providing a foundation that will reach below the frost line is one of the factors adding to the cost of a greenhouse planned for a cold area; however, such a foundation would add to the permanence and appearance of the building in any part of the country. Once built, the foundation will pay for itself in lower maintenance and heating costs for the whole structure.

One of the more economical—and space-saving— greenhouse designs is the leanto, built against one wall of a house. Here, of course, the cost of building a foundation is reduced because of the pre-existing wall.

The prospective greenhouse builder will find that many companies selling prefabricated greenhouses indicate foundation requirements along with their other instructions.

HEATING   Another factor influencing the cost of a greenhouse installation is, of course, heating. Perhaps the idea of heating another separate structure, or even an attachment to an existing building, has frightened many gardeners away from greenhouses in these days of higher fuel prices. We'd like to reassure you—it probably won't cost as much as you expect! We'll take a detailed look at heating requirements and how they can be met in a later chapter. But for now, keep in mind that most plants don't like it as warm as you do, and that the sun will provide a great deal of heat—especially if you've double-layered your window area by using an inner sheet of transparent

These small leanto and large even-span greenhouses are examples of the extraordinary variety of sizes and designs available. (Courtesy J. A. Nearing Co.)

Here are examples of the two most popular materials for greenhouse frame construction—redwood and aluminum. (Aluminum greenhouse photo courtesy Aluminum Greenhouses, Inc.; Redwood greenhouse photo courtesy Peter Reimuller—The Greenhouseman)

plastic during the winter months. Furthermore, the installation of a leanto-style greenhouse will allow heat from the home to help meet plant-growing needs. (It will also allow the gardener to visit his indoor garden without wearing a coat and boots!)

OTHER MAINTENANCE EXPENSES   The expense and personal involvement necessary for maintaining a greenhouse, once it has been built and stocked, depend on such variables as size, varieties of plants being grown, and the degree to which the gardener has installed mech-

Here is a serviceable and attractive greenhouse foundation siding made of asbestos board.

This leanto greenhouse has been insulated with a layer of transparent polyethylene film.

This economical leanto has been built onto a sturdy cinder-block foundation. Costs were reduced by use of pre-existing house wall at one side. (Courtesy Lord & Burnham)

anized equipment to take care of watering, ventilation, and temperature control. Devices that will perform all of these chores automatically are available, although their advisability (with the possible exception of a reliable thermostat) is questionable in the smaller home installation. The time spent puttering in the greenhouse could be reduced to but a few hours a week—but this is an unlikely problem to worry over, since the gardener will wish to spend as much time there as he can.

The expense of maintenance will be in direct proportion to the amount of care originally taken in erecting the greenhouse, or in the selection of a prefabricated model. A sturdy foundation, a tight glazing job, wooden parts treated or painted where necessary to minimize weather damage—all of these factors will help keep maintenance to a minimum.

First, be sure all metal strips are locked securely in place; second, place gasket firmly onto glass, and finally, fit glass snugly into opening. (Courtesy Lord & Burnham)

Chapter 2 SELECTING THE RIGHT GREENHOUSE

You've decided to build a greenhouse. What kind will it be? As we've seen, cost will be a limiting factor for all but the very few. But other considerations should also enter into your decision. Not the least of these is the extent to which you practice your hobby. A retired person, or a person whose schedule allows ample free time—provided this free time is matched by a devotion to gardening—will probably want as large a greenhouse as he or she can afford. Those with less time on their hands, or those not yet ready for a full-scale commitment to indoor gardening, will be much better off with a more modest installation, even if budget is no object. The novice gardener, faced with an oversized greenhouse to fill, might become discouraged by the challenge in time and effort, and fail to realize the potential enjoyment of a more easily managed unit. And although smaller greenhouses are more prone to inside temperature fluctuations, requir-

ing closer thermostat watching, it is foolish to heat too large a space if it will be underutilized.

On the other hand, it would be unwise to select a greenhouse solely on the basis of one's present requirements. Gardening is a hobby with a limitless possibility for expansion, as anyone knows who has experimented with cuttings and seed plantings. Therefore, it would be wise to choose a greenhouse that will allow for a reasonable amount of expansion, without undue crowding of plants.

Fortunately, there are prefabricated "sectional" greenhouses on the market that will provide such expansion—by the addition of compatible extension units. At least one supplier of prefabricated aluminum greenhouses advertises a permanent record-keeping service, enabling the manufacturer to offer perfectly compatible expansion sections to his customers at a later date.

Overhead view

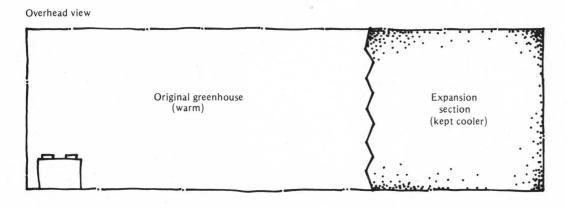

One of the advantages of a sectional greenhouse is the ability to provide two temperature ranges—for different types of plants—under the same roof.

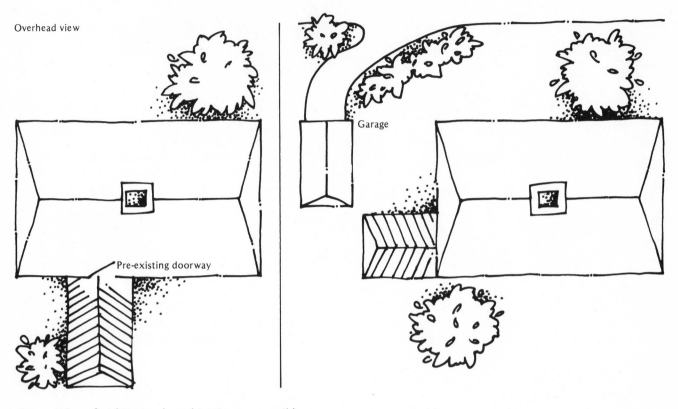

Overhead view

Garage

Pre-existing doorway

*Any number of architectural combinations are possible—
but plan ahead if you feel you may extend your greenhouse
some day.*

Later chapters in this book will indicate which styles of greenhouses are most capable of accepting future additions. Keep in mind that greenhouses installed upon permanent foundations will require extension of these foundations if further sections are to be added.

KEEP THE SURROUNDINGS IN MIND

Several other factors will exercise influence upon greenhouse size and design. These are the amount of land available upon which to build, and the type of structure, if any, to which the greenhouse is to be attached. If the greenhouse is to be a free-standing model—that is, one that is not connected to any other building—the size of your property will be the only space limitation. If, however, the new unit is a leanto model abutting the wall of a house, the builder must take the design of the house itself into consideration. Is there a convenient door that can be incorporated as an access to the greenhouse, or a window that can be enlarged to serve this purpose? Will the new greenhouse obstruct any entries, windows, or

significant architectural features of the house? Will future expansion be possible without running into any obstructions? Extensive or complicated redesign of a home to accommodate a built-on greenhouse can defeat one's purpose in choosing an inexpensive, easily built structure.

Fortunately, the greenhouse is much more often an asset than a liability as a companion to the home. Models are available in styles that will complement virtually every type of architecture; and in the event that yours is a home with special requirements, many suppliers offer consulting services and tailormade installations.

HOW HANDY ARE YOU?

Of course, size and appearance of the finished product are only part of the story. As with any do-it-yourself project, the time and degree of difficulty involved in construction are also points to be considered.

For many home gardeners, the choice between a greenhouse built from scratch and one put together from a kit is based upon how handy they are with tools. Since

Even-span greenhouse.

future satisfaction and ease of maintenance depend in large part upon the craftsmanship that goes into the building, a wise gardener will carefully take stock of his own abilities and act accordingly. If he or she has been successful with other home building projects, such as remodeling a kitchen or bath, finishing a basement, or putting a small addition onto the house, the home owner may want to start a greenhouse from scratch—using plans such as those provided by the U.S. Department of Agriculture, examples of which are reprinted in this book. This person should have a sound familiarity with hammer, saw, and glazing tools, along with an eye for detail and an attention to close tolerances: Chinks or cracks written off as "too small to worry about" now will mean added fuel expenses later.

So—if you plan to work from plans using your own materials, don't overestimate your skills. And give yourself enough time to do the job right.

The prospective greenhouseman who chooses a prefabricated structure will have a less demanding task ahead of him. In addition, reputable greenhouse suppliers stand behind their products, taking responsibility on those rare occasions when Part A and Part B don't fit together like the instruction sheet says they should. And often, a screwdriver is all you'll need in the way of tools.

The common denominator for the kit builder and the complete do-it-yourselfer is usually the foundation. Here's where a professional is usually required, particularly if concrete is to be poured or bricks are to be laid. Again, most instructions accompanying kits will tell exactly what sort of foundation, if any, is required. Be sure to follow these recommendations to the letter in working with a mason or concrete contractor.

Prefabricated or start-from-scratch? They both have their advantages. One offers the security of a guarantee, while the other offers a seasoned craftsman the challenge of a project intimately linked with his other hobby—gardening.

TYPES OF GREENHOUSES

Most people, if asked to visualize a greenhouse, would probably conjure up a mental picture of a glass building, straight-sided, with gabled ends and a gently sloping roof. This is the greenhouse professional growers usually favor, and it appears in scaled-down versions in many backyards and in virtually all of the literature furnished by home greenhouse manufacturers. Its popularity is by no means unwarranted; but it is only one of a myriad of greenhouse designs. Many of these designs were unheard of just a few years ago. Many have been made possible by new developments in materials or by revolutionary engineering discoveries.

Two categories

Basically, the full-sized structures we usually have in mind when we say "greenhouse" fall into two general categories: free-standing and leanto. Let's first take a look at the free-standing models.

FREE-STANDING   A free-standing greenhouse does just that: It stands free. Without attachment to another building on any side, it's obviously the greenhouse that

Examples of two free-standing greenhouses. (Courtesy of Sturdi-built Manufacturing Company)

This is a Dutch-style greenhouse, recognizable by its sloping sides. (Courtesy Lord & Burnham)

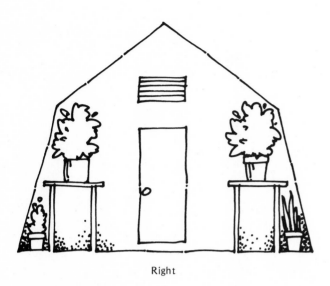

Right

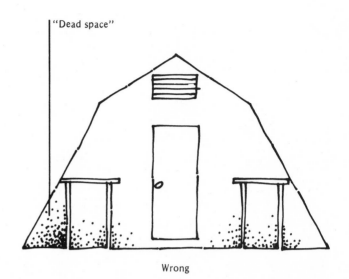

"Dead space"

Wrong

This "dead-space" effect is created by walls built at the wrong angle to the ground.

The quonset is a spacious, uncluttered design which lends itself well to covering with plastic film. (Courtesy Lord & Burnham)

will receive the most sunshine. Not that this doesn't have its disadvantages (remember our winter gardener trudging through the snow), especially since it requires a completely separate heating system. But for many amateur greenhousemen it's the top choice for spaciousness, sunlight, and ease of ventilation.

Among free-standing greenhouses there is a further subdivision of categories: the "even-span" structures, and those designs that incorporate less symmetrical shapes.

"Even-span" refers to the ground-to-rooftop uniformity of height at both ends that is characteristic of this style. Its basic representative is the standard greenhouse referred to earlier, with a symmetrically pitched, gabled roof and straight sides. There may be a variation of this last element, with the side walls splayed out somewhat in what is called the Dutch style. The advantages cited for this variation on the even-span design include, in smaller greenhouses, improved proportions; and among greenhouses of all sizes, a possible increase in the amount of winter light allowed in. Walls with a slope that is too flat, however, will create dead space near the floor—space useless for growing ground-level plants because of the limited headroom above.

Another departure from the traditional even-span principle is the "Quonset" greenhouse, named after the long, rounded "Quonset huts" hastily set up as military barracks during World War II. A Quonset-style greenhouse resembles a half-buried barrel, lying on its side. The more flexible covering materials, such as fiberglass and the plastic films, are especially suited to this type of greenhouse design.

A rounded-eave greenhouse. (Courtesy Lord & Burnham)

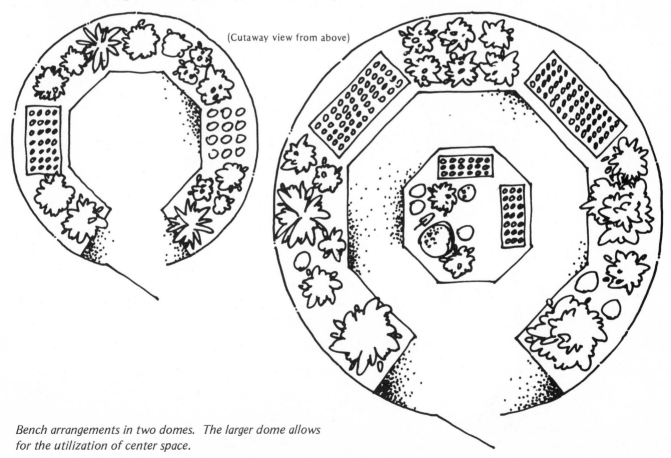

(Cutaway view from above)

*Bench arrangements in two domes. The larger dome allows
for the utilization of center space.*

The use of aluminum framing in some of the prefabricated even-span models permits a rounded-eave effect. Once again, the pliability of fiberglass comes into play here, as corrugated sheets of fiberglass are often installed along the roof and around these curved eaves as a shadowing device.

A-Frame, as described in text.

UNUSUAL DESIGNS   The free-standing, noneven-span greenhouses are in the realm of 'truly innovative design. Perhaps the most striking of these are the geodesic domes. They are built on the same design principles as the larger domes that are being constructed in many places for use as houses. The same features that make the dome some people's idea of an ideal home design contribute to its appeal as a greenhouse. Domes are light and, because of the equalization of pressure at stress points, sturdy. They are easy to construct, whether from plans or from one of the increasingly available geodesic kits. The design is adaptable to a variety of building materials and, because of its structural strength, is conducive to a favorable ratio of opaque-to-transparent materials. This ratio is a matter of concern in all greenhouse designs. Simply put, it refers to the area of nonlight-transmitting surface (i.e., framing materials) compared to the area of the surface which allows light to pass through —the greenhouse windows, or "lights," as they are called.

The dome-style greenhouse, of course, will call for a different arrangement of plant benches inside. A large enough dome will permit some central growing area as well as the benches along the perimeter of the structure.

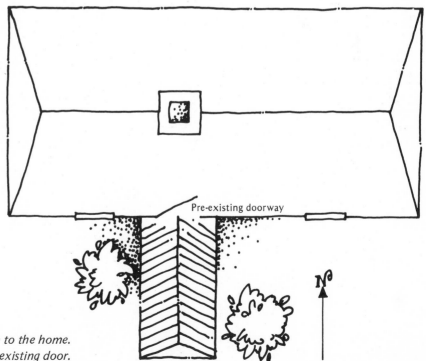

Pre-existing doorway

A simple method of attaching an even-span to the home. Entrance is most commonly through a pre-existing door.

As with all designs, it is important to allow sufficient room for the gardener as well as for the plants. It's no fun squeezing your way between the benches in a poorly planned interior layout.

The A-frame, a modern design, also will appeal to those with an eye for something different. This is another style that has been borrowed, like the dome, from larger buildings. One prefabricated model, designed by its manufacturer for quick installation without a permanent foundation, can be equipped with wing-like shades, which extend perpendicularly to the greenhouse walls near the peak of the roof. This is a novel approach to shading, particularly suited to this type of construction.

The possibilities for unusually shaped free-standing greenhouses may be quite limitless. While the clear plastic bubble has not yet been priced down to the average buyer's market, perhaps it will be in a greenhouse design of the future. The sheer, spherical styling would of course have to be altered, to allow for shading, ventilation, and access. These are imperatives for all greenhouse designs.

ATTACHED MODELS   Now we come to the attached greenhouses—those models which, in addition to easier access, offer closer proximity to existing sources of heat, electricity, and water.

Among attached greenhouses, the nearest compromise between the above-mentioned virtues and the advantages of the even-span style can be accomplished by simply butting one gable end of such a structure against a wall of the existing building. Here you have the convenience of an entry from the house, along with a three-sided exposure to the sun. If you are contemplating any future expansion of the greenhouse, this style will probably suit your purposes best. The addition of future segments will be a simple matter of expanding outward, away from the home, with no concern about preexisting architectural barriers. Another advantage borrowed from the free-standing type is the double entry—many gardeners install doors in their attached even-span greenhouses at the gable end opposite their homes, providing both freer ventilation and a ready access to other garden areas.

But perhaps the most popular of all attached greenhouses is the leanto. This style shares the length of one of its sides with the house, garage, or other existing building. In certain situations, where the design of the house creates a right-angled recess, the leanto greenhouse may be attached to both walls. But builders wishing to take advantage of such an arrangement had best consider the amount of sun that will be allowed to reach the remaining two glass walls: if only a northern exposure remains, constructing the greenhouse in such a nook would be poor economy indeed.

Generally, then, a leanto greenhouse is one that resembles an even-span model cut in half lengthwise and butted against the house. Those models in the seven- to twelve-foot width range, equipped with a central walk and a double row of benches, are in the least expensive

In addition to providing ready access to the outdoor garden, this two-door design facilitates ventilation within the greenhouse.

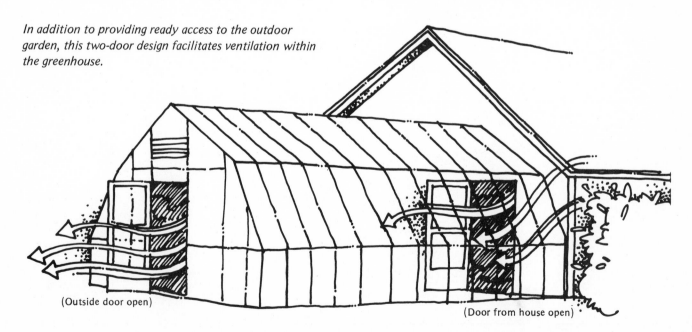

(Outside door open)

(Door from house open)

Air circulation (arrows) through greenhouse with 2 doors

category of greenhouses, whether built from plans or purchased in kit form. Any narrower adaptation of the leanto style would result in too severe a limitation of growing and work space. (Remember also that this estimate of the leanto's relative inexpensiveness is based upon cost alone; were we to figure in terms of lowest cost per square foot of growing area, the seventeen or eighteen foot even-span greenhouse would come out way ahead. It will accommodate not only side benches, but a center bench and double walkways as well.) Still, if

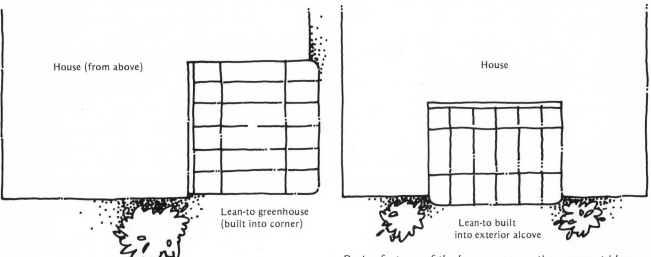

Design features of the home can sometimes suggest ideas for leanto installation—but make sure you have enough light!

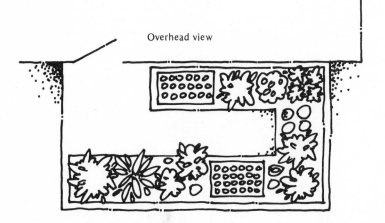

The amount of bench space available depends on the width and design of the greenhouse.

This unusual greenhouse not only offers a spacious solarium effect on the first floor, but even extends to an upstairs window. (Courtesy J. A. Nearing Co.)

located in an area that receives maximum sunlight, the leanto is a fine choice for gardeners concerned with accessibility and the cost of utilities.

VARIATIONS ON THE LEANTO   A pleasing adaptation of the leanto design can be accomplished by opening an entire wall of the home to the greenhouse. This serves a double purpose: It vastly expands the size and feeling of roominess in a den or informal living room, and it virtually brings the outdoors—with all its greenery and sunlight—right into the home. Before undertaking such a major alteration to your house, of course, it would be wise to determine the weight-bearing responsibility of the wall in question. Similarly, city gardeners who plan to

perch a leanto (or any other design) atop a roof or protruding lower story should see to it that the roof is either strong enough to begin with, or that it is reinforced to support the new load. A fully equipped greenhouse, even a smaller model, involves considerable weight. Before undertaking any such project, of course, apartment dwellers should get permission from the owner of the building. Fire codes, as well as a determination of what constitutes a "permanent addition," will sometimes come into play.

Other popular leanto installations include a basement-access setup, feasible where a sloping homesite has allowed for a ground-level basement at the rear of the

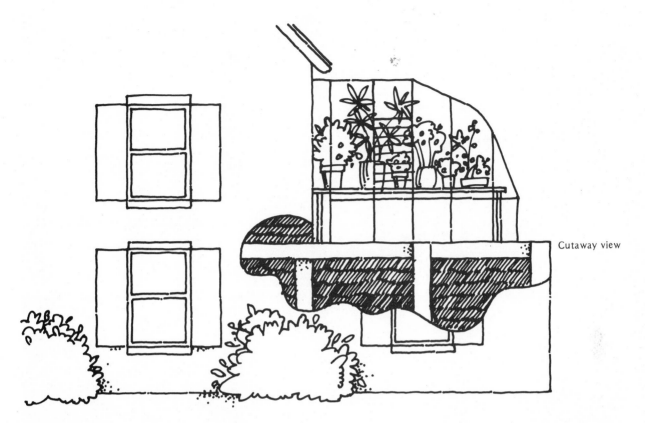

Cutaway view

Adequate structural support is necessary whenever a heavy, permanent structure is to be built onto a roof.

Second story greenhouse built onto back porch.

This gardener has installed his leanto so that access is from a basement family room.

Here are three window greenhouse installations—a single, a double, and an expansive picture window size. All three show proper position of window greenhouse shelves. (Courtesy Lord & Burnham)

house. In this application, the greenhouse foundation is dug to the level of the basement floor, and a door or simple passageway added. Although such a greenhouse has a full foundation, with complete protection against frost damage, the glass partition commences nearer to the outdoor ground level, allowing full room for growing without obstruction of the upper portion of the house.

WINDOW GARDENING   Maximum sunlight, along with minimum space and a more modest commitment to greenhouse gardening, make up the recipe for one of the most popular recent developments in glassed-in home horticulture—the window greenhouse. The window greenhouse is really an adaptation of the old windowbox; but it's a windowbox designed for year-round enjoyment. Many suppliers of full-size prefabricated greenhouses are now offering these easily attached units, and some will even custom-design installations to fit unusually shaped windows.

Basically, a window greenhouse is an aluminum-framed extension of the window itself. The sashes are removed from the window frame, allowing free access to the glassed-in area. Better models include a slanted, movable top, which can be propped ajar to allow air to circulate through an inner screen. Wire racks are placed inside the frame at required intervals for the types of plants being grown.

Another feature found in high-quality window greenhouses is a provision for placement of insulation in the bottom platform of the unit. Such models are provided with a hollow, double bottom for this purpose—the buyer fills this space with fiberglass batting in order to reduce heat loss. Window greenhouses—especially those fitted with a heavy, tight-fitting glass—rarely cause more heat loss than the windows they replace.

One striking application of window-greenhouse design is the multiple unit, shown above. Suppliers of quality kits, such as the manufacturer cited in the accompanying caption, have designed their window greenhouses so that they can be coupled (or tripled or quadrupled) with similar units to form this picture-win-

(left) Overcrowding of plants on shelf. (right) Properly spaced plants in window greenhouse.

dow greenhouse effect. The effect of such an arrangement in visually enlarging a room is amazing. One note of caution, however: couplings of window greenhouses work best in situations where a window, or series of windows, is already in existence. Otherwise it will be necessary to determine the extent to which wall areas that are to be broken through actually bear the weight of upper stories. This is a job best left to an architect or engineer, unless the present occupant of the house has direct knowledge of its original structural design.

What are the disadvantages of a window greenhouse? The most important of these might be the temptation to crowd plants within the unit; too many plants placed on the shelves will inhibit the free circulation of air and heat. Also, placing plants too near the glass walls of the window greenhouse might result in some winter damage. Keeping these precautions in mind, it would be wise to stock the window unit with plants that enjoy room temperature, and that are prone to low growth. African violets would be one excellent choice.

Other likely plants for inclusion in the window greenhouse are members of the herb family. Most of the herbs commonly used in cooking can be grown with little difficulty in small flats. Among these are the leaf-bearing herbs basil, thyme, savory, marjoram, and peppermint; and the seed herbs dill, fennel, coriander, and cumin. Herbs are generally hardy plants requiring only a moderately rich soil (in fact, over-nourishment would make them too unwieldly for the window greenhouse) and at least six hours per day of full sunlight. They will not demand special attention, although careful thinning and trimming for use will keep them from becoming overgrown and unattractive.

If the window greenhouse is properly stocked and attended to, there can be no better (or less expensive) addition to a window in a kitchen or breakfast nook that receives plenty of sunlight. It's a guaranteed "good morning" every day of the year.

Coldframes and hotbeds

Although they are not quite greenhouses, there are certain applications of the gardening-under-glass idea that deserve special mention because of their importance to

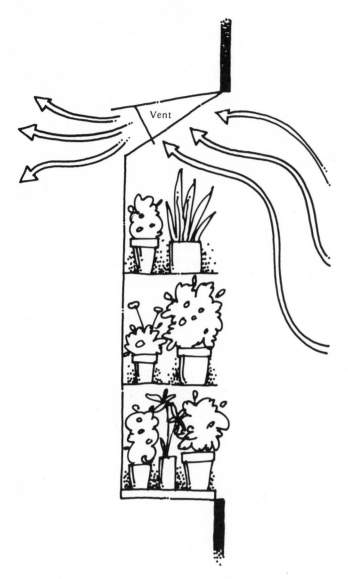

the vegetable grower and propagator of delicate seedlings. These are the coldframes and hotbeds.

COLDFRAMES Although both devices are similar in function and appearance, the coldframe is simpler than the hot bed. Both, also, can be either completely handcrafted or ordered in kit form.

A coldframe is really one of the most rudimentary —yet effective—applications of the solar heating principle. It is merely an open-bottomed casing, covered with a transparent material such as glass or fiberglass, which allows small plants growing inside to utilize the sun's heat, while protecting them from the cold winds and low temperatures common in the early part of the growing season. The soil inside the coldframe continues to give off absorbed heat during colder evening hours, making artificial heating unnecessary. Further insulation of this stored-up heat can be accomplished by banking straw, or straw mixed with manure, outside the frame.

What can you grow in a coldframe? For one thing, it's an excellent way to start vegetable and annual seedlings if you do not have a regular greenhouse, or are pressed for indoor growing space. The plants will grow to transplant-size under glass. Among other coldframe uses are the early-spring rooting of tree and shrub cuttings, starting of fuchsia and chrysanthemum cuttings, and warmer-weather cultivation of succulent and African violet cuttings.

FRENCH INTENSIVE GARDENING Vegetable gardeners interested in the use of coldframes would do well to look into a high-yield growing technique developed in the last century, known as "French Intensive Gardening."

Air circulation pattern in the window greenhouse.

Coldframe covered with hay

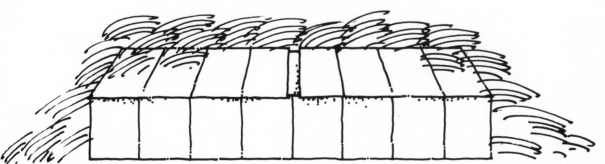

When temperatures are still low, the coldframe and its contents can be insulated by means of straw banking.

Originally introduced as a method of obtaining an extraordinary abundance of vegetables from a very small plot, the system involves trenching around the soil to be planted, and then cultivating and fertilizing the soil to depths of as much as a foot—in effect, creating a raised vegetable patch with superior soil aeration and nutrition. Coldframes are sometimes used in conjunction with this method, providing intensive sunlight to accompany the other idealized growing conditions.

HOTBEDS   The hotbed is a coldframe with a source of artificial heat added. This may simply be manure, which gives off a surprising amount of heat when it is confined and allowed to decompose. Other possibilities are steam or hot-water pipes extended from the house or greenhouse, or electric heating cables. Like the coldframe, the hotbed is of considerable use to the gardener who wishes to start seeds before it is time to plant them outdoors. Of course, the presence of artificial heating makes the hotbed viable even earlier in the season than the coldframe. After seedlings have gotten off to a healthy start in the hotbed, they may either be transplanted directly outdoors or, if an intermediate stage is desired, "hardened" without being moved, simply by cutting off heat and converting the hotbed into a coldframe.

Heating requirements for hotbeds, as well as construction details for both hotbeds and coldframes, will be provided in a later chapter.

In this treatment, the roofs of the house and greenhouse combine in a continuous slope. Note the roller shades drawn up near the peak of the greenhouse roof. (Courtesy Lord & Burnham)

The brick foundation of this attached even-span integrates the greenhouse with the home. (Courtesy Lord & Burnham)

A simple aluminum-frame leanto that takes up a ▶ minimum of backyard space. (Courtesy Lord & Burnham)

A well-stocked window greenhouse.

This leanto greenhouse makes the adjacent patio an even more attractive summertime gathering place.

This dome design allows the gardener ready access to all bench areas. (Courtesy Sturdi-built Manufacturing Company)

Hanging baskets make efficient use of greenhouse space.

Mesh shelving will not block light from plants growing below.

Ridge vent in open position, releasing hot, stale air on a summer day. ▶

Ample provision for ventilation marks this compact leanto. (Courtesy W. Atlee Burpee Co.)

A film-covered leanto such as this can be installed in one day. (Courtesy Turner Greenhouses)

This leanto is built to be entered from the basement of the home. Although the lights are of glass, plastic film has been added as insulation.

Clear glass panes allow indoor and outdoor gardens to harmonize. (Courtesy Lord & Burnham)

A "Dutch," or gambrel-roofed, fiberglass-panelled greenhouse. This installation has been made in a well-shaded area; plants with a preference for subdued light should be given preference here. (Courtesy Turner Greenhouses)

A simple yet effective interior layout. Note dual exhaust fans, which draw air through louvres (not shown) at opposite end. (Courtesy Turner Greenhouses)

The space in this greenhouse has been carefully apportioned. Note below-bench storage of soil bins, extra pots, and equipment. (Courtesy Sturdi-built Manufacturing Company)

A small even-span, attractively set amidst outdoor plantings. (Courtesy Sturdi-built Manufacturing Company)

Shading panels of redwood slots shield this greenhouse from excessive sunlight. (Courtesy Sturdi-built Manufacturing Company)

This combination wood and aluminum frame greenhouse
rests on a low concrete foundation, giving a glass-to-ground
effect beneficial to plants growing below bench level.
(Courtesy Texas Greenhouse Co.)

A high foundation offers added protection in areas of heavy snowfall. (Courtesy Lord & Burnham)

When cold weather comes, outdoor flowers can be potted and brought into the greenhouse.

These Burpee "Pixie Hybrid" tomatoes are especially suited for greenhouse growing. (Courtesy W. Atlee Burpee Co.)

A concrete block foundation.

A simple plastic drainpipe installation.

A gravel floor is practical as well as attractive. Puddles are avoided, and the wet stones release moisture into the air for hours after watering.

Easily-installed metal clips hold glass panes in place on this small even-span greenhouse.

This type of shade may be selectively installed and adjusted to allow sunlight to enter where it is desired.

These inside-mounted shades operate much like home window shades.

Ventilation louvres on a large plastic-film greenhouse.

This plastic film-covered even-span, shown resting on a concrete block footing, is among the easiest to install—yet it offers full protection. (Courtesy Turner Greenhouses)

Fine weather will induce the greenhouse gardener to show off his plants outdoors as well as indoors.

Chapter 3 BUILDING THE GREENHOUSE

GENERAL OBJECTIVES

In the previous chapters, we've discussed the architectural features and personal influences that should be considered when choosing a greenhouse location. While these factors are certainly important, there is one ultimate priority in greenhouse design that outweighs all others. In the simplest of terms: while the gardener may *prefer* a certain location for his greenhouse, his plants *demand* a location that suits their purposes. Now, this is not as harsh a dictum as it may seem; the gardener, after all, can exercise some choice over the type of plants he wishes to grow, and not all plants have the same sunlight requirements. Some decidedly prefer shade; indeed, this is a requirement for all plants during at least part of the day. But unless the new greenhouse gardener has a passion for mushrooms, he must select a site accessible to sunlight—preferably morning light. Don't forget, the sun is not only the major source of nourishment for plants, but it is also a considerable source of heat for the greenhouse. While all sorts of devices can be rigged up to lower temperatures and shade plants from excessive sunlight, there is little that can be done to alleviate a shortage of sunlight. So the cardinal rule of building greenhouses remains: *Build where the sun is best.*

Choosing the sunniest spot

A free-standing greenhouse, obviously, will receive sunlight from every direction, particularly if it is situated far enough away from other buildings. Building the free-standing even-span so that its narrow ends face north and south will give the structure the best exposure to both morning and afternoon sunlight, and will also minimize the amount of surface exposed to cold north winds. If an accessory workroom is to be built onto the free-standing greenhouse, it should be situated at the northern end. This will provide even greater wind protection for the glassed-in area.

If the separate greenhouse is to be built relatively close to the house, it would be advantageous to locate it in the southern lee of the larger building, where north winds will be most effectively broken. A greenhouse built on this location will also receive the greatest amount of light as long as there are no sun-blocking obstructions flanking its own southern exposure. Given such obstacles, the eastern, or especially the southeastern, exposures will be acceptable alternatives.

The attached greenhouse is likewise best placed at the southern, southeastern, or eastern exposure. As we have seen, winter light is most abundant on the southern side, but the morning light from the east is also important. This is because of the "biological clocks" in your plants, which regulate their growth and productivity. This regulation provides for maximum activity during morning hours; naturally, the light plants receive during these hours is most important to them. Plants' energies dwindle later in the day, so that afternoon sunlight will not benefit them as much. But a west-facing greenhouse, if it is the only possibility, need not be ruled out—flowers and plants will grow there, if not quite as enthusiastically.

Take trees into account

Nearby buildings are not the only possible obstructions to the sunlight required by plants. Trees are the other significant barrier, and if they are tall enough they can bar low, slanting winter sunlight even if located as much as 50 feet away. Evergreens, with their year-round dense foliage, create a poor environment for the greenhouse in nearly

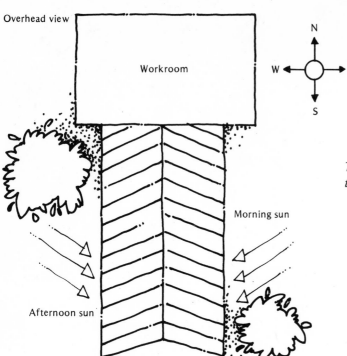

The greenhouse built on a north-south axis gets the best of the morning sun.

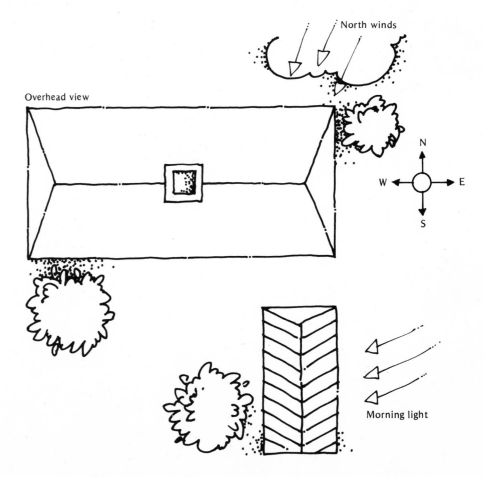

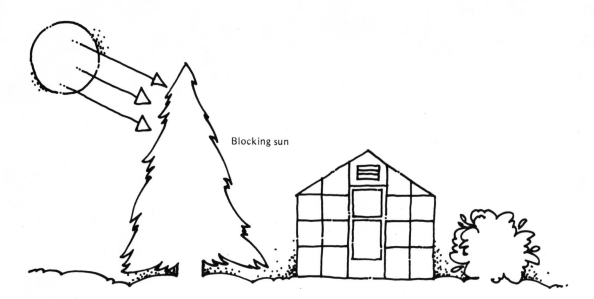

Dense evergreens, even seemingly distant ones, can screen or completely block precious light in winter.

all instances, but deciduous trees can serve the gardener's own purposes if they grow to the west of the greenhouse, where afternoon sun is most intense. During the summer, when they are in full leaf, these hardwoods will shade your cultivated plants. When they lose their leaves in winter, they will allow much-needed light to pass through their branches.

A word about trees growing too close to the greenhouse: in autumn, falling leaves will be a problem as they collect on the glass roof and clog drain facilities. Also, there may be a risk of falling branches damaging the greenhouse. If nearby trees are a part of the picture, they had best be pruned periodically—especially dead or weak branches.

Snow, ice, and hail are also threats to the greenhouse. While there is little that can be done about hail (primarily a problem in the midwest) other than using the strongest of glass or, better yet, fiberglass, there are precautions the gardener can take against snow and ice damage. If the greenhouse is a leanto or attached even-span model situated beneath an eave of the house, it would pay to install snow deflectors on the overhanging roof. This will keep accumulating snow from tumbling onto the glass below. Where icicles threaten from projecting gables or eaves, a possible solution would be to run an electric heating cable along the edge of the roof above the greenhouse—even if such a device is not in use along the rest of the roof. In terms of electricity costs, this is a small price to pay to prevent icicles from building up and

eventually dislodging, perhaps to come crashing against the greenhouse glass.

What about the snow that falls on the roof of the greenhouse itself? If the roof has been given the correct pitch, the snow should slide off without any difficulty. If you live in a heavy snow area and are ordering a greenhouse kit, be sure that the model you choose has a healthy slant to the roof. The same advice applies to plans for do-it-yourself building, some of which are designed with northern winters in mind. If you intend to use USDA Extension Service plans, such as those offered in this book, select those developed at University Experiment Stations in snow-belt states. The selections printed later in this chapter reflect design research conducted in various locations.

Should you be going it entirely on your own, however, or if you wish to modify the design of an existing plan, the most commonly prescribed pitch for an even-span roof is 6 in 12, which means that for every 12 inches of roof slope, there is a rise of 6 inches. This will create a pitch of about 27 degrees.

Design proportions

There are other building proportions equally helpful to the greenhouseperson, whether designing an original structure or evaluating published plans or prefabricated models. A properly proportioned greenhouse has a height equal to the eave height (distance from ground

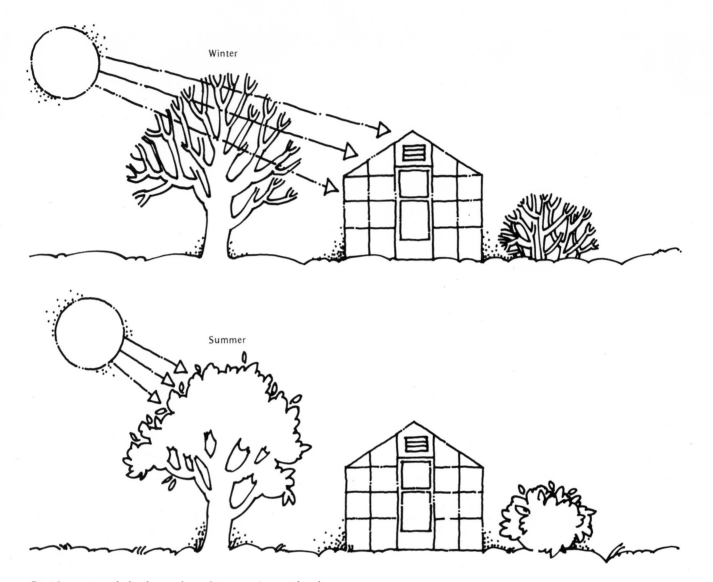

Deciduous trees help the gardener by screening out harsh light in summer, but permit slanting winter rays to shine through.

to eave) plus one-fourth of its width. Gardeners favoring low-growing plants usually prefer an eave height of about 5 feet, although taller varieties may require an extra foot or two. Be sure to consider the type of plants you want to grow when you shop for a greenhouse kit or consider plans.

Manufacturers' kits will generally be proportioned in order to accommodate the type of benches provided by that manufacturer, in the amount specified for the particular model. Most leantos, for instance, are designed to house two benches—one along the pre-existing house

wall, and one along the outer wall. Many smaller even-span models follow the same arrangement, although wider designs, as we saw in the last chapter, allow space for a central bench. If you are providing your own benches for a prefabricated greenhouse, it is important not to exceed the manufacturer's bench-size recommendations, lest crowding result.

Plant benches placed along the walls should, of course, be no wider than the gardener's arms are long. Those placed along the center may be twice as wide, since they can be approached from both sides. What

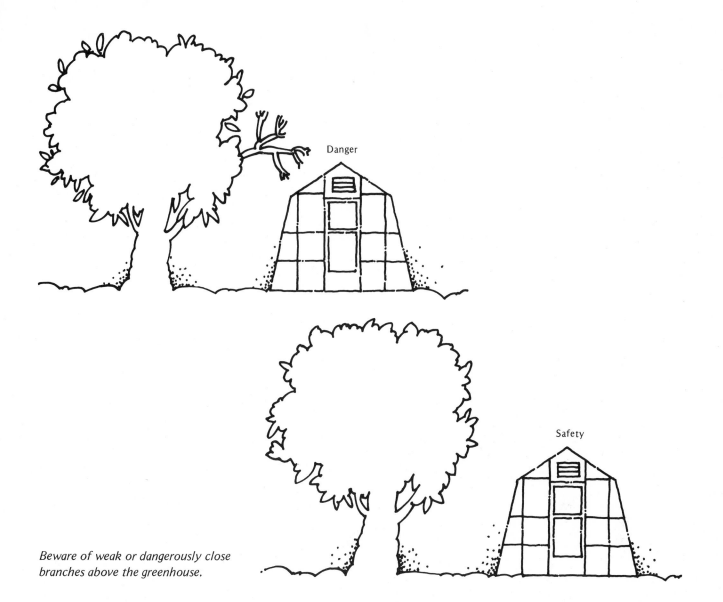

Danger

Safety

Beware of weak or dangerously close branches above the greenhouse.

about the paths between? A width of 18 or 19 inches should be sufficient, unless a wheelbarrow is to be used between benches, or unless visitors will frequently accompany the gardener into the greenhouse.

These factors taken together—plus an allowance for at least two inches of air circulation space between outer walls and benches—will govern the width of the building. Width, in turn, will have a direct effect on the desired height. Length, as we have seen, depends primarily upon the number of plants to be grown and the space available for building. And unlike width or height, it can always be modified later.

PREPARATION OF THE SITE

The final considerations of greenhouse layout relate to the characteristics of the ground at the site. First, the ground should be level. If it is not level, this can be corrected during the digging and construction of the foundation. But if yours is to be a small, light greenhouse, without a full foundation, a careful leveling of the ground is vital not only to esthetics but to sturdiness and convenience. The second variable associated with the building site is drainage. The disadvantages of a low, boggy site are obvious, but poor underground drainage is also unde-

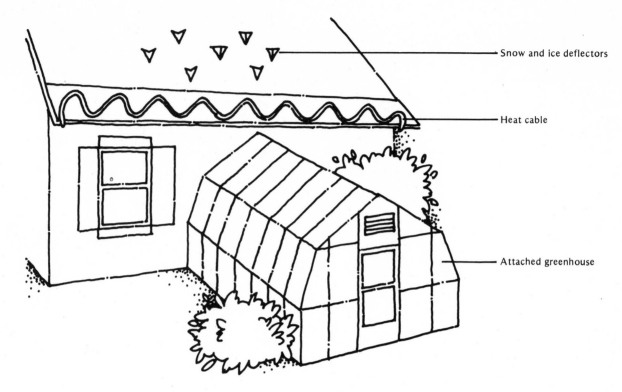

Snow and ice deflectors

Heat cable

Attached greenhouse

Ice deflectors and heating cables are valuable allies in the battle against winter damage to greenhouse glass.

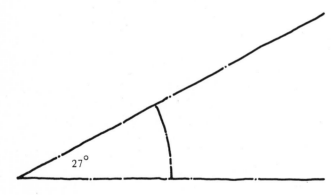

27°

The proper pitch of a greenhouse roof.

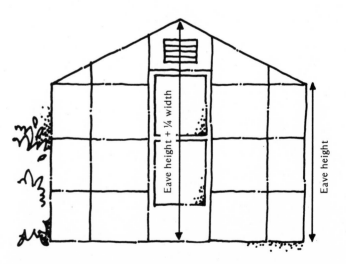

Proper height-width proportions

Eave height + ¼ width

Eave height

These are the most harmonious proportions for an even-span greenhouse.

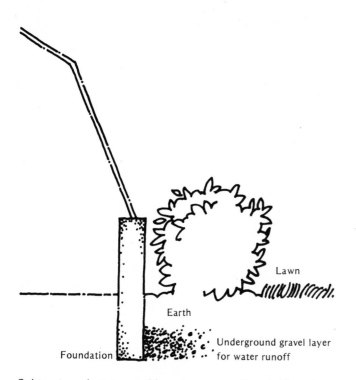

Solve minor drainage problems by surrounding the foundation with an underground layer of gravel at the time the greenhouse is built.

Aluminum frame members in kit greenhouses are easy to assemble, produce strong joints.

sirable. Such a situation can be corrected by providing gravel or perforated tiles for runoff when you build your foundation.

BUILDING MATERIALS

Now we come to the real substance of the new greenhouse. What materials should be used? This is an important question, not only for the do-it-yourselfer following plans, but also for the gardener in the prefabricated market, since different manufacturers claim different virtues for the various materials that go into their kits. And not without reason. Each substance that goes into modern greenhouse components has proved its worth in one way or another; each also has drawbacks which competitors say will be avoided if the consumer chooses *their* alternative. We will now take a look at major construction materials, starting with frames.

At one time, nearly all greenhouses were built with wooden frames. The tendency of many woods (especially untreated woods) to rot or warp, combined with the obstruction to light inherent in a heavy wooden frame, made this a less than ideal solution. Iron- and

steel-framed greenhouses followed, and these can still be seen in commercial enterprises where sturdiness is the principal requirement. For the backyard gardener, however, structures of iron or steel will seldom be practical. There are certain exceptions, one of which is a pipe-frame used to give shape to a plastic-film greenhouse inflated with air. This project is discussed in a brochure published by the U.S. Department of Agriculture, entitled "Building Hobby Greenhouses." But for most gardeners, iron-pipe construction will probably be limited to plant benches.

Two leading materials

The two major trends in greenhouse framing today are redwood and aluminum. Nearly all of the kit manufacturers emphasize one or the other of these materials.

Aluminum, while somewhat more expensive at the time of construction than any of the woods, is unbeatable for durability. It surpasses even steel, which must be painted to inhibit rust. It is certainly the lightest of the popular framing materials, and aluminum frame members occur with minimum frequency in a greenhouse design because of their favorable strength-to-size ratio, allowing for a greater transparent surface area. Aluminum is also easy to work with since it is available in sections designed for greenhouse building. These, like the members provided in prefabricated kits, simply bolt together.

There is, however, one drawback to aluminum: it is an excellent conductor of heat, and as such it will draw heat out of the greenhouse and dissipate it into the outer air. This will be a minor consideration in warmer climates, but in areas where artificial heat must be provided for a good part of the year, the prospective buyer should question the aluminum frame supplier as to what the estimated heat loss will be in the model under consideration.

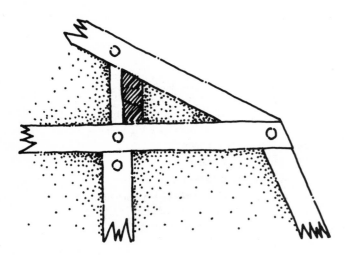

Frame members of quality redwood greenhouses are bolted together, rather than secured with nails or screws. Look for this feature when shopping for prefabricated models.

Redwood is the most popular alternative. It is one of the most rot-resistant woods, possessing a natural acidic quality that inhibits fungus growth and decomposition. It is strong, with a dense grain that resists splintering and milling irregularities. But as with less durable woods, it is best to treat it with a preservative, such as copper naphthenate. The manufacturer may already have provided this treatment, should you be ordering a prefabricated redwood greenhouse; find out from him if it has already been treated. When treating the wood yourself, avoid creosote or pentachlorophenol—they are harmful to plants.

Although the preservative treatment is advisable, redwood differs from other woods, even from superior and expensive cypress, in that it does not require painting. It does, however, require the use of hot-dip galvanized nails and screws, since its natural preservative acids corrode unprotected metal.

Other possible choices for wooden framing include fir and red cedar, both of which should be selected—as should redwood and cypress—from straight-grained, knot-free, kiln-dried stock. Both of these woods should be treated with copper naphthenate, then double-coated with paint (special greenhouse paint is available from garden supply houses and better hardware stores). This paint will have to be renewed every few years, especially since periodic scrubbing is recommended in all greenhouses for the control of algae.

The chief advantages of wood are its lower initial cost, non-conductance of heat, and retention of atmospheric humidity. In a purely esthetic vein, many people consider it the most beautiful of greenhouse framing materials. Its disadvantages primarily center upon the care required to avoid its deterioration. Redwood, however,

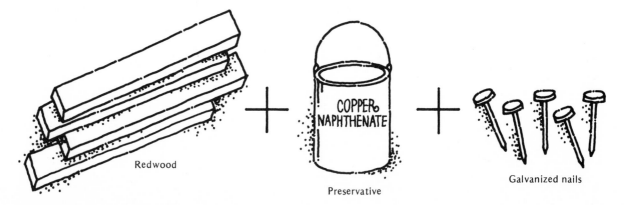

Redwood   COPPER NAPHTHENATE   Galvanized nails
                    Preservative

Even redwood will last longer if treated—and don't forget to use galvanized nails on this naturally acidic wood.

Glass greenhouses, emphasizing transparency.

is highly rot-resistant and needs less attention than other woods.

Glazing

The most important construction factor comes in the glazing, or selection of "lights," as the transparent parts of the greenhouse are called. Without lights, there would be no light—it is as simple as that. But glazing is no longer a job for glass alone. There are a myriad of transparent and translucent substances in use in greenhouses today. Glass, though still a leader, is no longer alone.

There are a number of convincing reasons for the survival of the glass greenhouse. The first is visual appeal —even its detractors frequently admit its beauty. Because it is *transparent* rather than merely *translucent*, glass allows the gardener a clear view of the outside and lets

This glass greenhouse is available with gable-end panels and door panes of shatterproof glass and acrylic.

outdoor viewers enjoy the colors of the garden growing within. Another advantage of glass is its unchanging appearance. While plastics can be prone to scratching and fading, a clear pane of glass will remain so indefinitely.

Gardeners wary of glass greenhouses generally cite fear of breakage. While no one can guarantee that glass —at least the affordable glass used in greenhouse construction—will *never* break, manufacturers have come up with resilient varieties that stand up well against the elements and an occasional misdirected football.

Use the best materials

The key to safety and peace of mind in glazing a greenhouse is to remember that ordinary window glass will not do the job. The type of glass you'll want generally goes by the name of "double-thick," with a weight of at least 24 ounces to the square foot. "Single-thick" glass seldom exceeds 16 ounces per square foot in weight, and is much less likely to stand up to hailstones, which are perhaps the greatest single threat to glass greenhouses. Even if you live in a part of the country seldom troubled by hail, double-thick glass is the wisest and sturdiest choice.

Certain imperfections in glass, such as waviness and variations in thickness, have been known to create a "lens" effect, damaging the foliage of plants exposed to the heat-intensive spots they create. Modern glassmakers have all but eliminated this problem. To be absolutely sure of the quality of the glass you buy, deal with a firm specializing in greenhouse glass.

Glass quality, of course, is also a consideration in the selection of a greenhouse kit. All reputable manufacturers use double-strength glazing, and some offer extra safety features. One supplier of prefabricated kits made in England advertises front panels and door panes made of shatterproof glass and acrylic.

Glazing the garden-size glass greenhouse is a project simple enough for the amateur to undertake. Kit manufacturers usually supply the necessary tools, and many have designed their products so that glass is held in place by steel clips or easily installed plastic flanges. Do-it-yourselfers using glazing compound are best off with plastic bead compounds, which resist later hardening and cracking. Follow the glazing instructions accompanying the particular plan you have chosen.

ALTERNATIVES TO GLASS   Glass, of course, has its rivals, and the most important of these is fiberglass. It has come into its own over the past decade both as a raw material for the plan builder and as a component of kit greenhouses.

Fiberglass is strong. What's more, it is light in weight (5 or 6 ounces per square foot) and adaptable to curvilinear greenhouse designs such as the Quonset. The panels are produced in sizes larger (widths up to 40 inches; lengths to 12 feet) than most glass panes; this, combined with their sturdiness, reduces the number of structural light barriers in the design.

The fiberglass most commonly seen in greenhouses is the corrugated, wavy-surfaced variety, although flat

Sturdy fiberglass greenhouse resists breakage. Ability of fiberglass to conform to contours also allows use of designs such as the gothic model shown. (Courtesy Texas Greenhouse Co.)

acrylic panels are beginning to make an impact on the prefab market. The translucent quality of most fiberglass is a definite drawback in terms of visibility, but fiberglass lights allow an adequate amount of evenly diffused sunlight to reach greenhouse plants.

Like glass, fiberglass comes in many grades and varieties, not all of which are suited to greenhouse use. Low-grade fiberglass will discolor, and this discoloration will consequently affect light transmission. Likewise, color-tinted fiberglass is a poor choice.

Even finer grades of fiberglass are prone to scratching and weathering, although some types may be refinished.

THE FLEXIBLE PLASTICS   A third category of greenhouse glazing materials share the light weight and ease of installation of fiberglass, but are cheaper than either glass or fiberglass. These are the flexible plastic sheetings, comprising a myriad of chemical compounds that vary

Plastic film will need occasional replacement, but it is unmatched for inexpensiveness and ease of construction.

considerably in their light-transmission qualities and durability. Even the finest of them, however, must be replaced periodically, and may be no match for a blustery winter in New England or on the Great Plains. For seasonal structures or in relatively temperate climates, however, they may be just the thing for the gardener concerned with fast construction and economy.

Polyethylene, vinyl (PCV), and mylar polyester are the most popular of these flexible coverings. Of the three, polyethylene is generally the least expensive, although its life-span is the shortest. Even if it survives winter snow and winds, it faces deterioration under the summer sun because of the action of ultraviolet rays. New varieties of polyethylene, treated against the harmful effects of these

rays, are available at a slightly greater cost. Their cloudy appearance will not inhibit sunlight transmission.

Films made of polyvinyl chloride (PCV) offer more than twice the longevity of polyethylene, at more than twice the cost. They are available in both transparent and translucent versions. Drawbacks include a tendency to attract dirt, and to contract with temperature changes. These films will become brittle when the mercury drops below zero, and are thus a poor choice for northern climates. Should you decide on vinyl, specify a fungus-resistant brand.

Mylar film is similarly long-lasting. Its strength must be matched by that of the greenhouse frame, since it should be stretched tight for optimum performance. (This

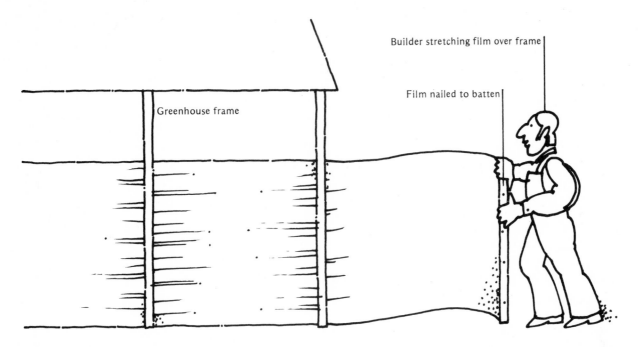

When greenhouses are to be glazed with plastic film, uniform tension can be assured through use of a wooden batten while installing. Taut application is especially important with mylar.

This gardener is putting the finishing touches on a film insulation job. Savings on fuel will be the result.

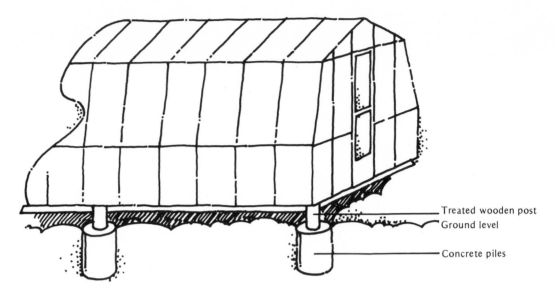

Treated wooden post
Ground level

Concrete piles

Posts anchored in concrete make a sturdy, easily constructed greenhouse foundation.

tautness inhibits the destructive and annoying "snapping" to which flexible plastics are prone in high winds.)

All of these plastic films are available in varying thicknesses—from as thin as 1.5 mil to 12 mil or more. Make sure to choose the thickness that best suits your requirements, and proceed carefully with the manufacturer's installation instructions. These will generally involve stretching the film over the frame by means of a wooden batten applied to one end of the unrolled film. The batten is used in order to provide equal stress at all points of the tightening film, eliminating sags and wrinkles. Similar battens are used over points where the plastic is fastened to frame members, thus reducing stress caused by nail holes.

The stronger films can also be used as coverings for coldframes, depending on whether heavy snow is expected to fall. Remember, also, that even the lighter varieties of polyethylene are valuable as inside winter linings in a glass greenhouse, where researchers have estimated that a 20 percent heat saving can be accomplished by creating a 2- to 4-inch-thick dead-air layer along outside walls.

Foundation requirements

The selection of framing and glazing materials can be entrusted to the kit manufacturer, should the builder decide to follow the alternative. But as we saw earlier, one task facing both the kit buyer and the gardener who builds "from the ground up" is that of providing the foundation.

The simplest greenhouse arrangements, installed in milder climates, will need no foundation beyond a careful leveling of the ground. But a permanent structure expected to survive unfriendly weather had best be given a solid footing. Whether you do the work yourself or assign it to a contractor, it will pay to familiarize yourself with the various materials and techniques used in building greenhouse foundations.

The simplest foundations are little more than anchor posts, made either of steel or treated wood, set into concrete or firm soil. These, in fact, are specified by some of the prefabricated kit manufacturers. These devices work well with light, modest structures, although the posts should be checked periodically for loosening and may have to be replaced every few years.

A true and permanent foundation requires some excavation and the use of masonry. The depth of the excavation will depend upon the depth of the frost line in your area. Three feet is generally adequate through most of the United States, although gardeners on the northern plains and in New England would do better to dig to a depth of four feet. This will assure freedom from frost-heave damage, which will be particularly unwelcome if the greenhouse is attached to another building.

If you feel that a deep foundation is unnecessary, you may still want to bury a length of corrosion-proof screening below the excavation line, in order to discourage burrowing rodents.

The above-ground height of the foundation wall depends on a number of variables. Obviously it should

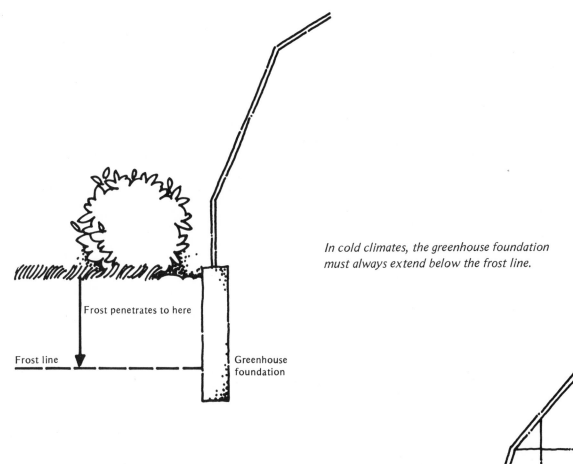

In cold climates, the greenhouse foundation must always extend below the frost line.

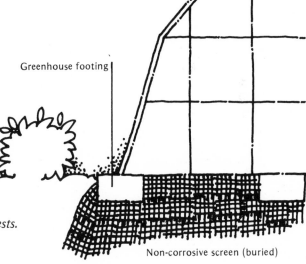

Underground screens will baffle burrowing pests.

not exceed the inside benches in height, or the plants growing on them will be denied a portion of sunlight. Also, decide whether you will be growing plants on the floor, below the benches. If so, 10 to 15 inches will be the maximum allowable wall height.

It is possible to erect a "glass-to-ground" green-house—that is, one which rests upon a foundation set deep into the earth but extending only a few inches above. Such a design offers a maximum of below-bench growing space, but it will cost a bit more to heat. Remember, also, the problem of accumulated snow pressure against the lower glass walls in northern climates.

(top) Limestone facing makes for a very attractive green-house foundation. (Courtesy U. S. Department of Agriculture)

(bottom) Glass-to-ground greenhouse. (Courtesy W. Atlee Burpee Co.)

POURING A CONCRETE FOUNDATION

There are several steps involved in laying a concrete foundation or footing. First, the building site is carefully marked off by the erection of temporary "batten boards" at the exact outer corners of the proposed foundation excavation. Next, the course to be followed by the concrete is excavated. For a greenhouse, hand shoveling will suffice, unless you are building in a northern climate where a substantial depth must be reached. If the excavation of such a trench would put too great a requirement on time or muscle, the services of a contractor with a backhoe might be required.

The next step in preparing the foundation excavation is to build the wooden forms into which the concrete will be poured, and in which it will harden. It is not necessary to frame the bottom of the excavation; here the concrete may make direct contact with the earth. Make sure to build the sides of the form up to the above-ground height required by the greenhouse you are building. This is also the time to consult the specific greenhouse plans with which you are working to determine if any anchor bolts or other hardware are to be inserted in the concrete while it is still wet.

Unless yours is an extremely small job, you will probably arrange with a ready-mix concrete firm to deliver the mixture to the site. When the truck arrives, work quickly and smoothly, preferably with one or two helpers, to guide the flowing concrete from the truck chute into the forms. If the forms you have built are level and true, the remaining work will primarily involve smoothing the wet concrete with a mason's wooden "float" and allowing it to dry completely before removing the forms and backfilling the area around the new foundation.

For a more detailed description of the processes involved in digging, pouring, and finishing building foundations, see *Build Your Own Home* by Robert C. Reschke (Farmington, Michigan: Structures Publishing Co., 1976).

View from above

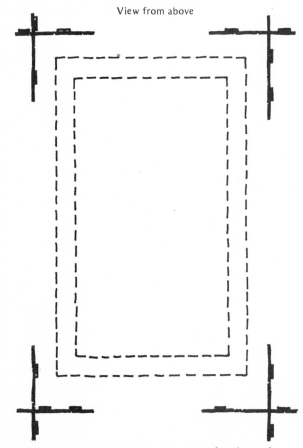

This dotted outline shows the course of a planned foundation of poured concrete. The batten boards marking the lines of the excavation and eventual foundation wall should be set up several feet back from the line marking the outer edge of the wall, but should be laid straight and true. If you can borrow a transit, it will help in marking these boundaries.

Side view (cutaway)

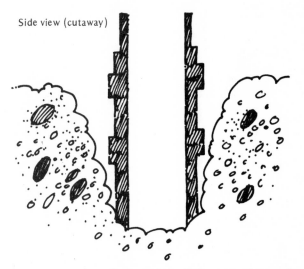

Cross-section of wooden forms into which concrete is poured

Here is a cross-section of the wooden forms used to guide poured concrete for a foundation. Note that the forms extend above the ground level. For a glass-to-ground greenhouse, this above-ground extension would be minimal.

(top) Single in-ground concrete block foundation gives glass-to-ground effect. (bottom) Layered concrete block foundation.

The materials most commonly used for foundations are poured concrete and concrete blocks. For esthetic purposes, the part of the foundation that extends above ground may be covered with stone, brick, redwood, or whatever other durable substance blends with the garden surroundings or architecture of attached buildings. Asbestos board and redwood siding are commonly used as surfacing for upper foundations, affording as they do both strength and insulation.

When undertaking a masonry project yourself, remember that your most important tools are not pick and shovel but plumbline and level. Any errors in leveling or trueness of line and angle will only be magnified as construction goes on, perhaps making it impossible to mount the finished structure.

Floors and walks

Once you've laid the foundation, you will add the greenhouse floor. What kind of floor do you want? No matter what type is selected, the first step in preparing the greenhouse floor is to smooth and tamp the ground. Some authorities even recommend removing surface soil, which may settle and sour, and replacing it with several inches of subsoil, gravel, or sand, which is then wetted and tamped. This may be unnecessary; if you are in doubt, consult a soil specialist at your state Extension Service.

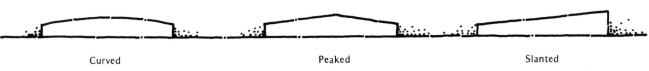

Curved   Peaked   Slanted

Concrete walks, when installed in the greenhouse, should either be banked or rounded to facilitate water runoff.

There is generally no need for a permanent floor in the greenhouse, unless it is an attached unit intended as a full extension of the house. A floor of stone or poured concrete, in fact, would hinder drainage unless a system of drains were installed.

An even layer of crushed stone is an ideal ground cover for the area under plant benches. It will not only drain water effectively, but will also store and release humidity. For walkways between benches, the gardener may prefer slats of a rot-resistant wood such as redwood; this is probably the most comfortable alternative. Others include flagstones, randomly chosen flat steppingstones, or bricks laid in wetted and tamped sand. Like the crushed stone, bricks store and release humidity.

The most durable and elaborate walkways are those of poured concrete. These can invite puddles and wet feet, however, if they are not designed to shed water. A sloped or crown construction is recommended.

Benches

Plant benches are the most important features inside a greenhouse aside from the plants themselves. These can be built to the gardener's own specifications, if not ordered ready-made; however, a few generalizations can be made concerning bench design and materials.

Plant benches are usually built at about table height —30 inches, more or less depending on the height of the gardener. They are best equipped with sides, so that either pots or soil may be placed in them, and they must allow adequate drainage. Cypress, redwood, and asbestos board are the preferred materials, although more common varieties of lumber will do if they are treated with copper naphthenate (such treatment will benefit the finer woods as well, but remember, do not use creosote or other chemicals harmful to plants).

The supports for benches need not be made of wood; indeed, perhaps the unnecessary use of a rare and valuable crop such as redwood should be discouraged here. Some of the most effective bench supports are constructed of iron pipe—galvanized iron, of course, because the supports will be exposed to a great deal of moisture. Other possibilities include concrete blocks or

30 in.

Benches are usually set about 30 inches off the ground—the height which an average-sized person finds comfortable for working.

precast piers, although these will be considerably heavier than the pipe frame.

WORKING WITH PLANS

Before donning work clothes and reaching for the toolbox, the builder should see to it that he understands the

The bench at left is being constructed of cinder blocks, while that on the right is of the more common pipe-frame and asbestos board construction.

rudiments of building from plans. A reacquaintance with building procedures and the use of basic tools might also be a good idea.

The U.S. Department of Agriculture plans which follow are drawn up according to standard architects' notations. This involves the use of scale drawings, whose purpose is to show the relative size of the various components of each greenhouse, and two principal types of two-dimensional representation: the floor plan and the elevation, or side view. Both of these viewing schemes, as well as variations on them drawn at different angles, are designed to show structural aspects of the building which would not be apparent in a picture of the finished product—for instance, the position of rafters or the method of affixing the building to the foundation.

All members of the frame, as well as the fixtures and surface materials, are accompanied by a notation of their length at least once in the series of drawings which make up a blueprint or plan. In addition, the length of a particular member will be noted separately on each side of its intersection with a second member. This, along with the use of exact scale, helps the builder visualize the relationship of parts in the whole. Where a construction procedure is to be duplicated, it is of course detailed only once in the plan.

Lines which are broken by a jagged edge, with their pattern resumed following this break, indicate that a deletion has been made. This is usually done to avoid duplication of instructions for an already-established sequence of construction details, although it could also indicate the exclusion of a feature detailed separately elsewhere. In

any event, remember that a drawing so abbreviated will no longer give a true sense of proportion—although full lengths of the "shortened" members will be noted.

Solid lines indicate visible outlines of structural components, whereas broken lines are often used to show the hidden edges of these components.

Builders following these plans will notice a full list of necessary materials accompanying the drawings, with the exception of instances in which the materials are few and have been itemized directly alongside those segments of the drawings outlining their use. Although substitutes can often be found for specified materials, there is no substitute for a thorough examination of these lists long before construction begins. Nothing is more frustrating than to be proceeding smoothly on a project, only to find that an item crucial to the next step is missing. If a particular fixture or material is unavailable, judge in advance how it can be replaced. Don't be forced to "fudge" a substitute with one hand while trying to keep everything from falling down with the other.

The same applies to tools. "Use the right tool for the job" may seem a shopworn adage, but there is no better advice when it comes to building projects. Go through your tools before starting the job—buy what you don't have, and sharpen and clean what you do.

Keep a clean and orderly workplace—try to keep it as clean and orderly as the blueprint itself; that way, the appearance of your project will bear some relationship to the drawings, and references will be easier to make.

The same rules apply to kits. Unpack everything first, and read the directions through before getting under way. If there is anything missing or damaged, call the supplier—don't try to make do without, or hope that a substitute whatsis will turn up in your basement. When the items you've unpacked begin to make sense in the light of the instruction sheet, then proceed. Never start building "right out of the crate," figuring on consulting the instructions only if something goes wrong. Something surely will.

With these construction ideas in mind, let's examine some of the greenhouse plans drawn up by the engineers of the U.S. Department of Agriculture Cooperative Extension Service.

SPECIFIC PLANS

Dutch-style greenhouse

We'll begin with a Dutch-style free-standing greenhouse (Plan 1). This plan, developed by Extension engineers in New Jersey, is reminiscent of the gambrel-roofed homes in that part of the country. The design, however, is a welcome one wherever a small (10' by 12') space must be put to the fullest use.

Note that this unit is designed to be covered with panels of corrugated fiberglass, with alternate instructions for an air-inflated flexible plastic covering. Note also that the supports for plant benches are an integral part of this greenhouse, bolted as they are to the main vertical members of the frame. Benches of the builder's choice may sit atop these supports.

The foundation specified is simple, consisting of 4" by 4" posts placed at designated intervals. A more elaborate foundation can of course be substituted. Redwood, in this case, is specified for the baseboard only, although builders having (or wishing to seek) access to this durable wood could use it throughout the frame (except for plywood gussets).

In following this and all other plans, make a careful study of the materials required before you begin. Should any of them be unavailable, or should you wish to make substitutions, consult your Extension agricultural engineer (addresses listed in Appendix C) regarding possible alternatives.

Gothic

Here is a "Gothic" greenhouse, which is yet another variation on the even-span principle (Plan 2). It is designed to be covered with plastic film. Its major frame members are double plywood strips, bent to meet at the ridge boards. Be sure to select clear, high-quality "exterior"-grade plywood.

This model is billed by its designers as "portable"; it is held fast to the ground by simple wooden stakes at the door frames and sides. Again, a heavier-duty foundation could be improvised, although this would detract from the structure's portability.

Tri-Penta

The Tri-Penta is a truly unusual design. It is a variation on the geodesic principle of adjacent triangular planes; these planes help share stress and their framework offers great transparency to light.

The foundation posts for this greenhouse are somewhat more permanent, and are set in poured concrete. The total diameter is approximately 16½'. (See Plan 3.)

Polyurethane film in a 6-mil-thickness is specified. Vinyl might be substituted, but mylar could be difficult to stretch to its optimum tautness over the irregular surface.

A special bench plan accompanies this design.

Framing for large greenhouse

Also included is a framing plan for a 48' greenhouse (Plan 4), with a 22' width that could easily accommodate a central plant bench. The plan's designers have indicated the possibility of expanding this into a 96' structure, although this would almost surely be too large for the average backyard. Forty-eight feet is itself no small affair, but we have included this plan to give some idea of the principles involved in constructing the larger units.

Glazing for this king-size greenhouse is pretty much up to the builder's discretion, although the choice had best be limited to fiberglass or plastic film. The use of glass would require further partitioning of the spaces between frame members with glazing bars and, because of weight and the disaffection between glass and frost, a full foundation.

Hotbeds

Shown in Plans 5 and 6 are two hotbeds which differ in design but not in basic function: both are heated by electric cables embedded in the soil, and both are designed to take full advantage of the slanting sunlight of cooler months. The peak-roofed model makes use of both wooden rafters and steel conduit to support its wire-mesh and plastic covering, while the domed version—a sort of mini-Quonset—employs sturdy wire mesh alone. Both, however, are to be glazed with plastic film.

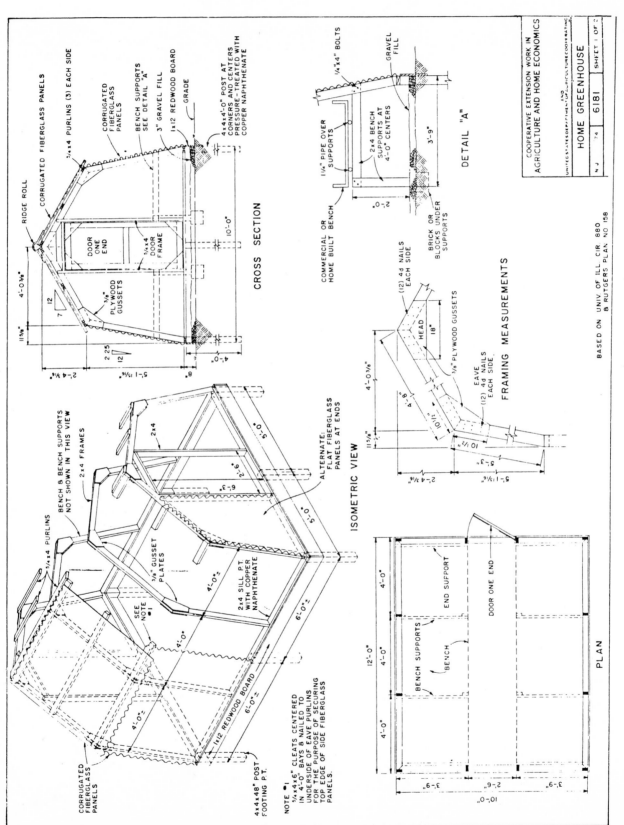

Plan 1(a)

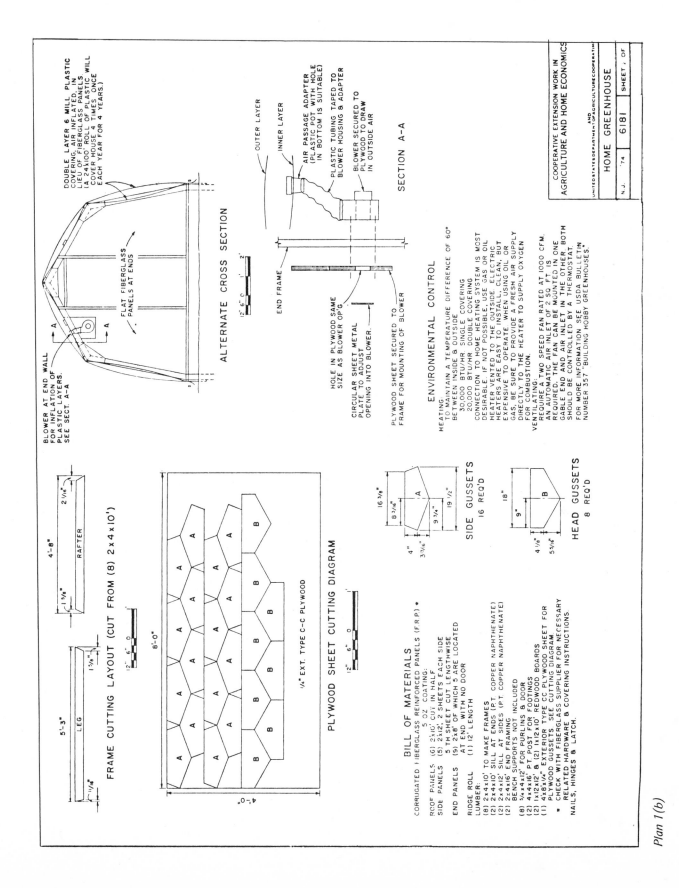

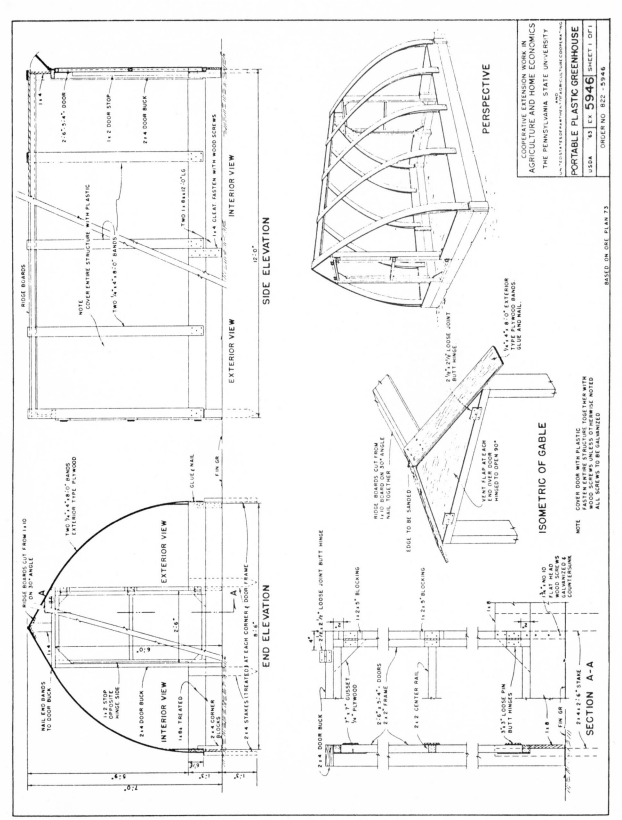

Plan 2

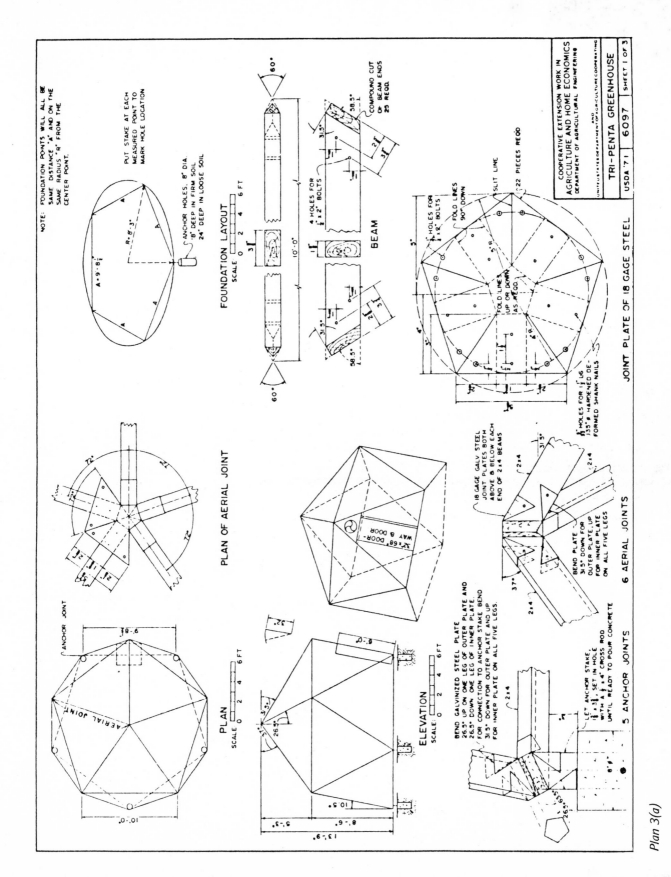

Plan 3(a)

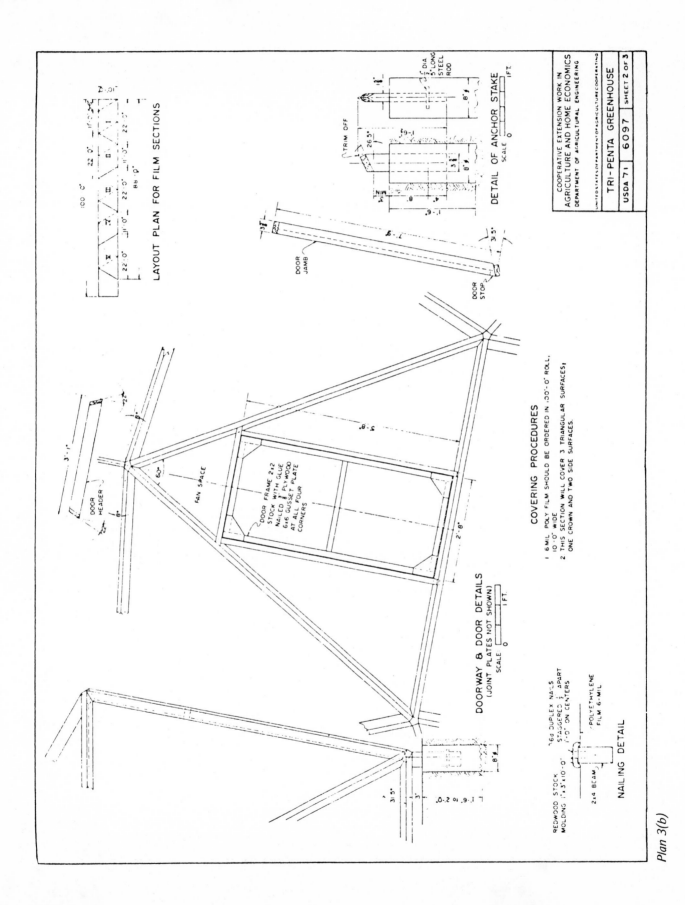

LAYOUT PLAN FOR FILM SECTIONS

DETAIL OF ANCHOR STAKE

DOOR JAMB

DOOR STOP

DOORWAY & DOOR DETAILS
(JOINT PLATES NOT SHOWN)

DOOR HEADER

FAN SPACE

DOOR FRAME 2×2 STOCK NAILED WITH GLUE ¾" PLYWOOD 6×6 GUSSET AT ALL FOUR CORNERS

COVERING PROCEDURES

1 6 MIL POLY FILM SHOULD BE ORDERED IN 100'-0" ROLL, 10'-0" WIDE
2 THIS SECTION WILL COVER 3 TRIANGULAR SURFACES, ONE CROWN AND TWO SIDE SURFACES.

NAILING DETAIL

REDWOOD STOCK MOLDING ¾"×3"×10'-0"

16d DUPLEX NAILS STAGGERED ¾" APART 1'-0" ON CENTERS

POLYETHYLENE FILM 6-MIL

2×4 BEAM

TRI-PENTA GREENHOUSE

COOPERATIVE EXTENSION WORK IN AGRICULTURE AND HOME ECONOMICS
DEPARTMENT OF AGRICULTURAL ENGINEERING
UNITED STATES DEPARTMENT OF AGRICULTURE COOPERATING

USDA 71 | 6097 | SHEET 2 OF 3

Plan 3(b)

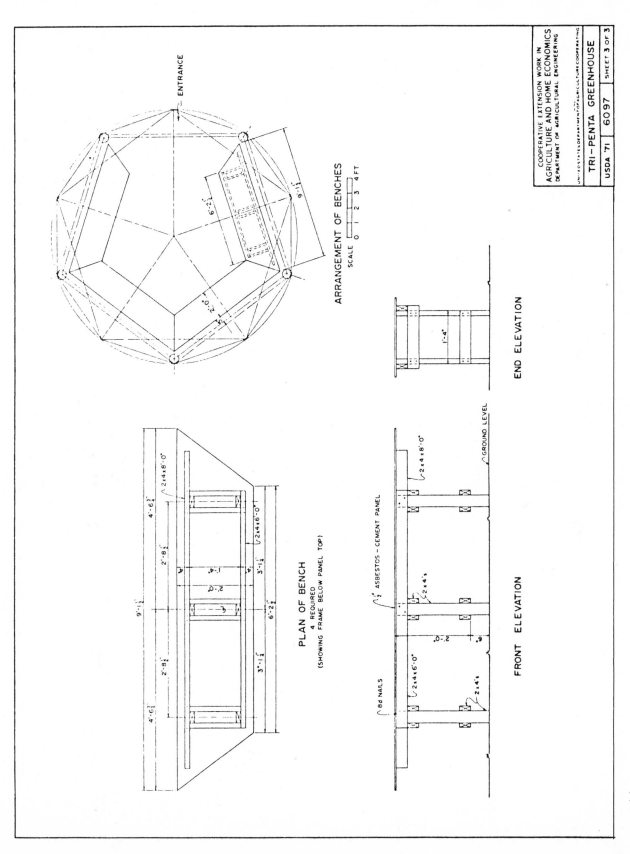

ENTRANCE

ARRANGEMENT OF BENCHES

SCALE 0 1 2 3 4 FT

PLAN OF BENCH
4 REQUIRED
(SHOWING FRAME BELOW PANEL TOP)

END ELEVATION

FRONT ELEVATION

COOPERATIVE EXTENSION WORK IN
AGRICULTURE AND HOME ECONOMICS
DEPARTMENT OF AGRICULTURAL ENGINEERING
UNITED STATES DEPARTMENT OF AGRICULTURE COOPERATING

TRI-PENTA GREENHOUSE

| USDA '71 | 6097 | SHEET 3 OF 3 |

Plan 3(c)

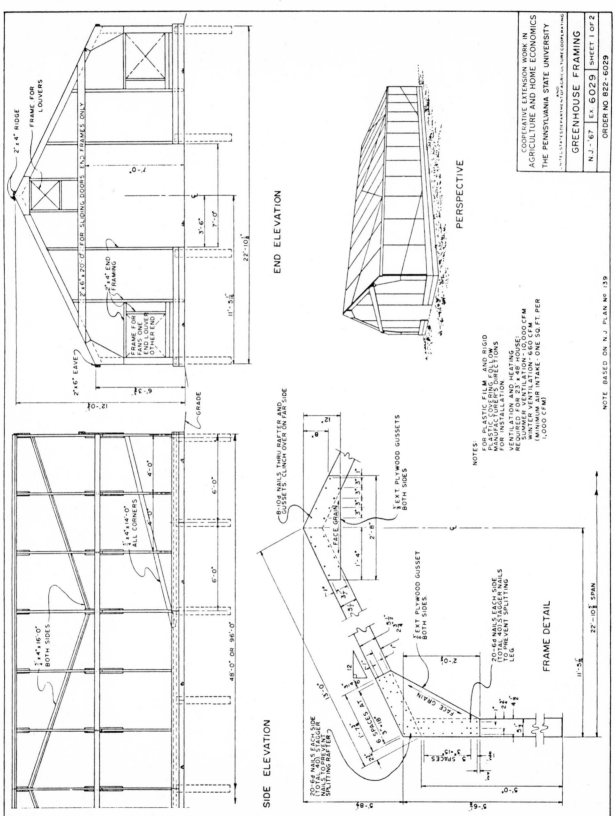

Plan 4(a)

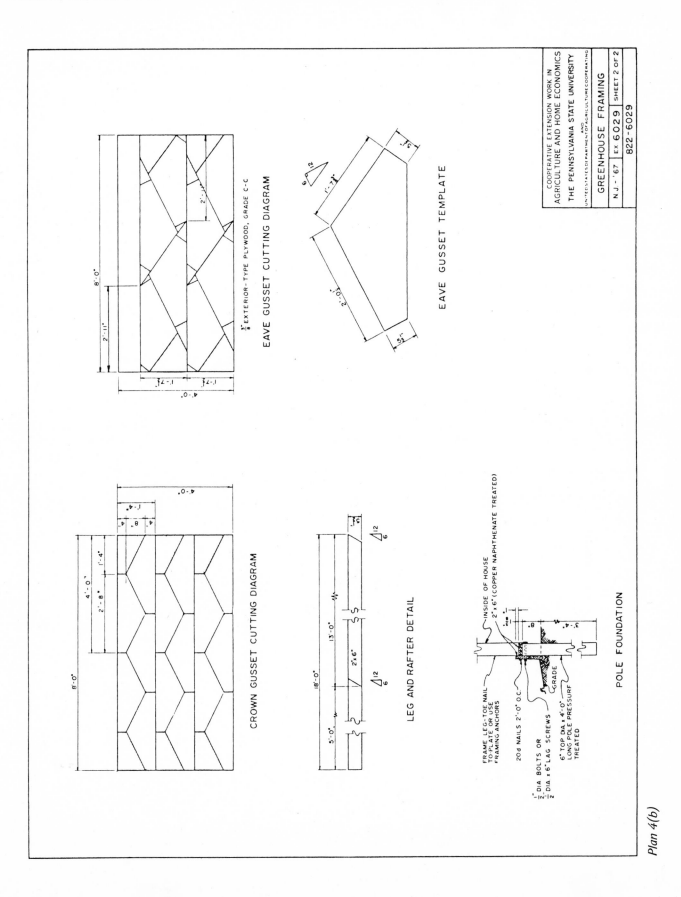

EAVE GUSSET CUTTING DIAGRAM

$\frac{3}{8}$" EXTERIOR-TYPE PLYWOOD, GRADE C-C

EAVE GUSSET TEMPLATE

CROWN GUSSET CUTTING DIAGRAM

LEG AND RAFTER DETAIL

POLE FOUNDATION

GREENHOUSE FRAMING

COOPERATIVE EXTENSION WORK IN
AGRICULTURE AND HOME ECONOMICS
THE PENNSYLVANIA STATE UNIVERSITY
AND
UNITED STATES DEPARTMENT OF AGRICULTURE COOPERATING

NJ-'67 | EX 6029 | SHEET 2 OF 2

822-6029

Plan 4(b)

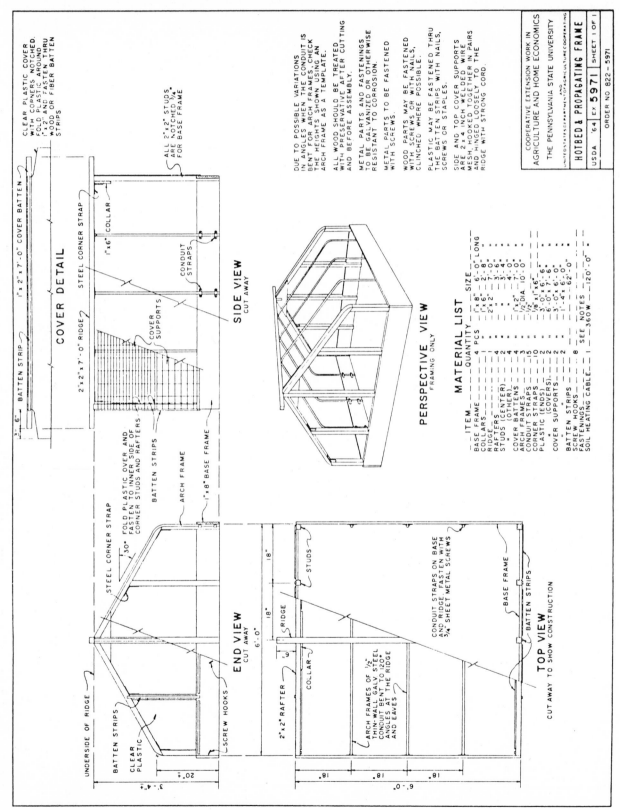

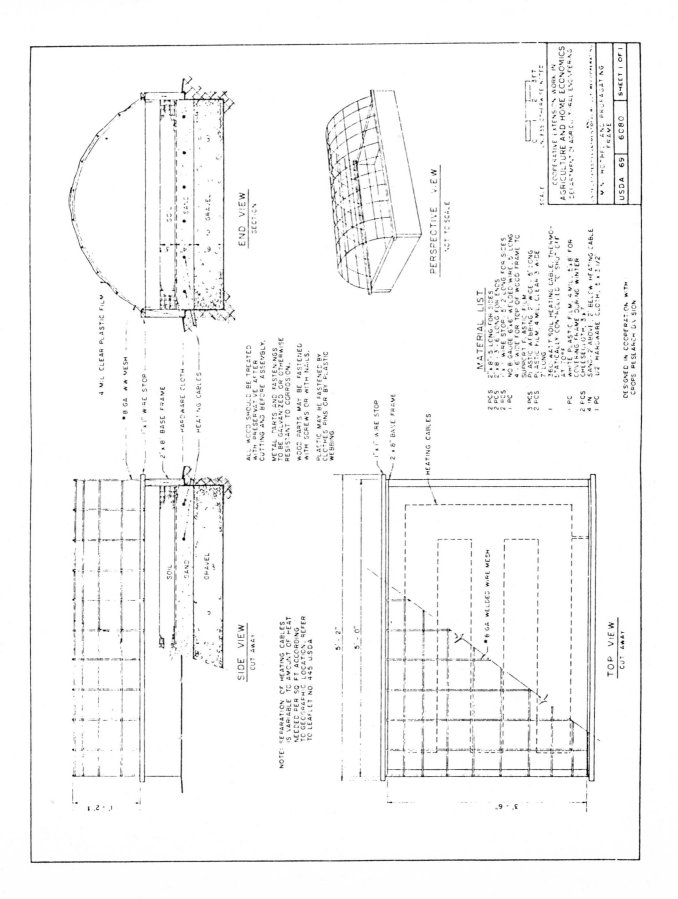

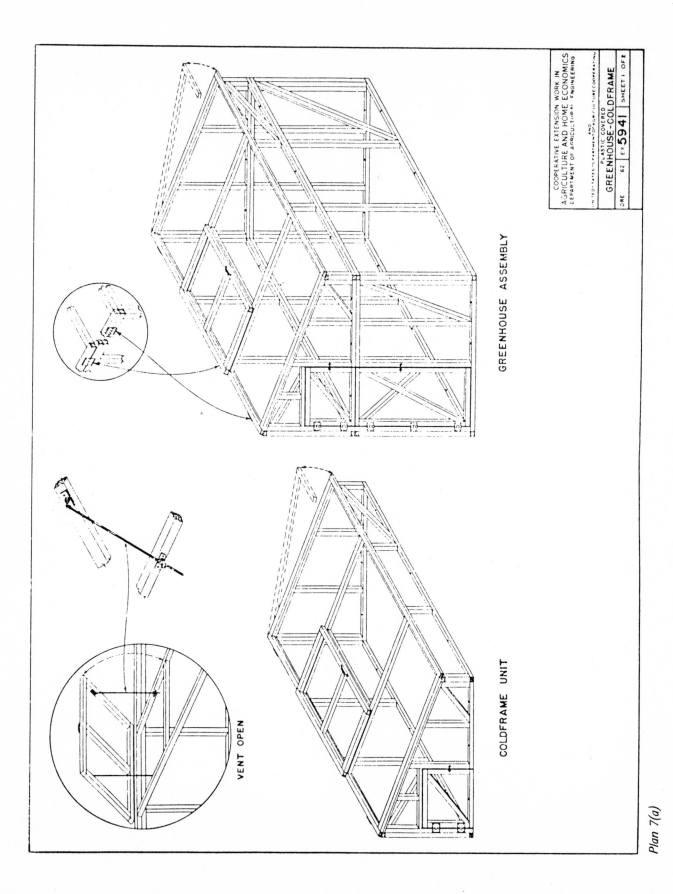

GREENHOUSE ASSEMBLY

VENT OPEN

COLDFRAME UNIT

COOPERATIVE EXTENSION WORK IN
AGRICULTURE AND HOME ECONOMICS
DEPARTMENT OF AGRICULTURAL ENGINEERING
AND
U. S. DEPARTMENT OF AGRICULTURE COOPERATING

PLASTIC COVERED
GREENHOUSE-COLDFRAME

ORE | 62 | EY | 5941 | SHEET 1 OF 2

Plan 7(a)

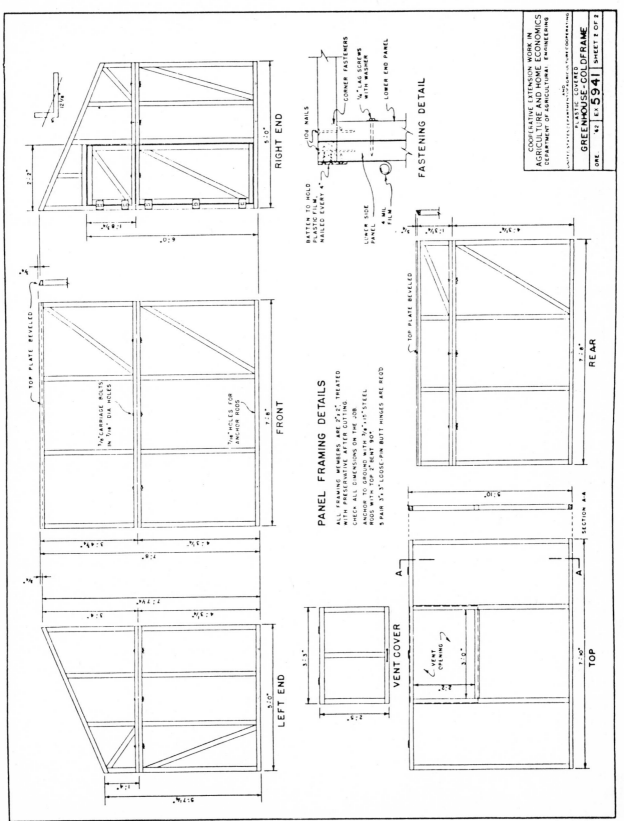

PANEL FRAMING DETAILS

ALL FRAMING MEMBERS ARE 2"x2", TREATED
WITH PRESERVATIVE AFTER CUTTING.
CHECK ALL DIMENSIONS ON THE JOB.
ANCHOR TO GROUND WITH 3/8"x15" STEEL
RODS WITH TOP 2" BENT 90°
5 PAIR 3½" LOOSE-PIN BUTT HINGES ARE REQ'D

FASTENING DETAIL

VENT COVER

RIGHT END

FRONT

LEFT END

REAR

TOP

SECTION A-A

COOPERATIVE EXTENSION WORK IN
AGRICULTURE AND HOME ECONOMICS
DEPARTMENT OF AGRICULTURAL ENGINEERING
UNITED STATES DEPARTMENT OF AGRICULTURE COOPERATING

PLASTIC COVERED
GREENHOUSE-COLDFRAME
ORE. '62 EX 5941 SHEET 2 OF 2

Plan 7(b)

CONSTRUCTION NOTES

GENERAL

SELECT A LEVEL, WELL DRAINED SITE.
PREFERRED LOCATION-SOUTH OR
SOUTHEAST, EAST, WEST.
PAINT POSTS, BENCHES AND LUMBER THAT
IS NEAR THE GROUND WITH THREE COATS
OF COPPER NAPTHENATE WOOD PRE-
SERVATIVE.

FRAME

USE CONSTRUCTION GRADE F.R. LUMBER.
PAINT FRAME WITH AN EXTERIOR WHITE PAINT.
DOOR CAN BE PLACED AT EITHER END.
USE FLASHING BETWEEN HOUSE WALL AND
GREENHOUSE ROOF.
CAULK ALL CRACKS.

COVERING

ROUND AND SMOOTH ALL EDGES
FOR SPRING AND FALL USE,
USE SINGLE LAYER OF 6 MIL POLYETHYLENE
PLASTIC HELD IN PLACE BY 1"x2" FIRRING
STRIPS.
FOR YEAR AROUND USE 2 LAYERS OF POLY-
ETHYLENE WITH UV INHIBITOR SEPARATED
BY A 2"x2" SPACER.
PLASTIC SHOULD BE APPLIED IN SEPTEMBER
OR OCTOBER.
5 OZ. CLEAR FIBERGLASS CAN BE USED AS A
COVERING TO REDUCE MAINTENANCE.

WALKS

A CENTER WALK OF PEA STONE OR
BRICKS LAID IN SAND CAN BE ADDED
AFTER THE GREENHOUSE IS BUILT.

VENTILATION

A 10 INCH DIAMETER FAN WITH AUTOMATIC
BLOWER AND THERMOSTAT SHOULD BE
USED.
LOCATE A 10 OR 12 INCH INTAKE LOUVER
ON OPPOSITE END WALL.
PLACE THERMOSTAT ALONG SIDE WALL
NEAR PLANT LEVEL.

HEAT

HEAT MAY BE SUPPLIED FROM THE
HOME HEATING SYSTEM OR FROM A
SEPARATE HEATER OUTPUT RE-
QUIRED CAN BE OBTAINED FROM
THE FOLLOWING TABLE.

	SINGLE LAYER PLASTIC OR FIBERGLASS BTU/HR			DOUBLE LAYER PLASTIC BTU/HR		
30°	8960	13780	17820	5940	9160	11900
20°	13780	17820	22360	9160	11900	15340
10°	17820	22360	26780	11900	15340	17800
0°	22360	26780	31200	15340	17800	20800
-10°	26780	31200	35750	17800	20800	23720
	50°	60°	70°	50°	60°	70°

MINIMUM OUTSIDE TEMPERATURE °F — MINIMUM NIGHT TEMPERATURE

1"x4" DIAGONAL BRACE

12'-0" 3'-0" 3'-0"

RAFTER 2"x4" 2"x3" FAN 2"x3" FRAMING SEE DOOR DETAIL

2'-0" 2'-0" 5'-1½" 3'-0" 8'-0" 2'-4" 2'-5"

6'-3" 8'-3" 8'-7"

SEE FOUNDATION DETAIL

COOPERATIVE EXTENSION WORK IN
AGRICULTURE AND HOME ECONOMICS
AGRICULTURAL ENGINEERING DEPARTMENT
UNIVERSITY OF CONNECTICUT
STORRS, CONNECTICUT
AND
U.S. DEPARTMENT OF AGRICULTURE COOPERATING

8'x12' LEAN-TO GREENHOUSE

Plan 8(a)

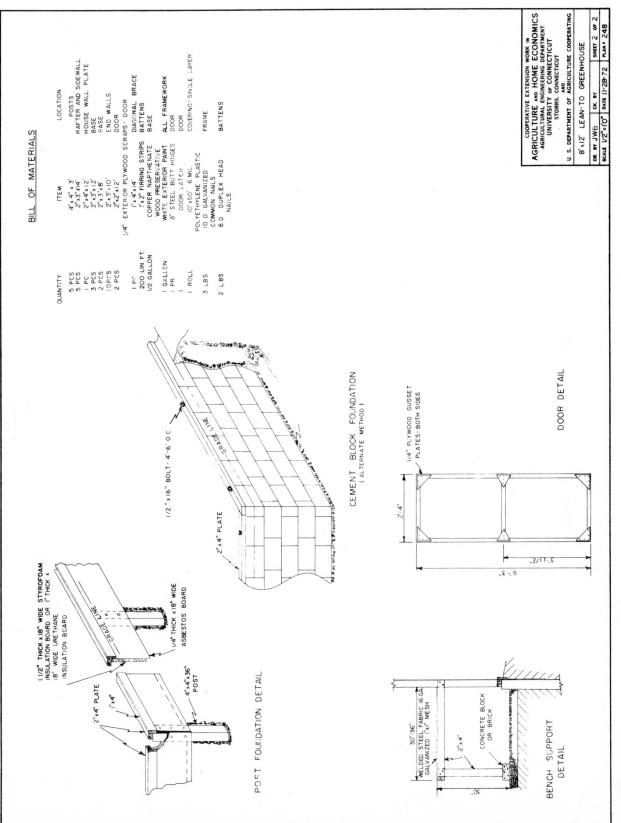

BILL OF MATERIALS

QUANTITY	ITEM	LOCATION
5 PCS	4"× 4"× 3'	POSTS
5 PCS	2"×3"×14'	RAFTER AND SIDEWALL
1 PC	2"×4"×12'	HOUSE WALL PLATE
3 PCS	2"×3"×12'	BASE
10 PCS	2"×3"× 8'	END WALLS
2 PCS	2"×2"×12'	DOOR
1 PC	1/4" EXTERIOR PLYWOOD SCRAPS-DOOR	DIAGONAL BRACE
	1"×4"×14'	BATTENS
200 LIN FT.	1"×2" FIRRING STRIPS	BASE
1/2 GALLON	COPPER NAPTHENATE	
	WOOD PRESERVATIVE	
1 GALLON	WHITE EXTERIOR PAINT	ALL FRAMEWORK
1 PR	3" STEEL BUTT HINGES	DOOR
	DOOR LATCH	DOOR
1 ROLL	10'×50' 6 MIL	COVERING-SINGLE LAYER
	POLYETHYLENE PLASTIC	
3 LBS	10 D GALVANIZED	FRAME
	COMMON NAILS	
2 LBS	6 D DUPLEX HEAD	BATTENS
	NAILS	

POST FOUNDATION DETAIL

CEMENT BLOCK FOUNDATION
(ALTERNATE METHOD)

DOOR DETAIL

BENCH SUPPORT DETAIL

COOPERATIVE EXTENSION WORK IN
AGRICULTURE AND HOME ECONOMICS
AGRICULTURAL ENGINEERING DEPARTMENT
UNIVERSITY OF CONNECTICUT
STORRS, CONNECTICUT
AND
U. S. DEPARTMENT OF AGRICULTURE COOPERATING

8'×12' LEAN-TO GREENHOUSE

DR. BY JWB	CK. BY	SHEET 2 OF 2
DATE 11-28-72	PLAN# 248
SCALE 1/2"=1'0"	

Plan 8(b)

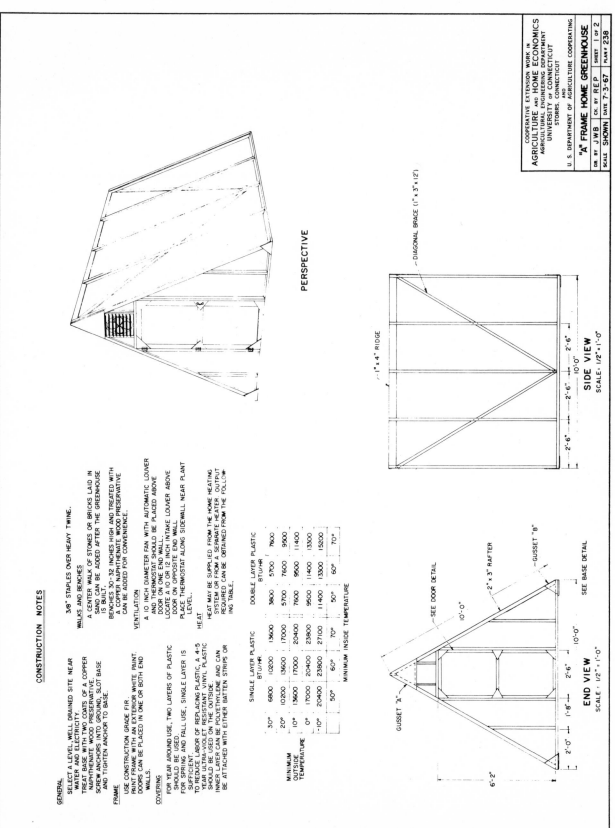

CONSTRUCTION NOTES

GENERAL

SELECT A LEVEL, WELL DRAINED SITE NEAR WATER AND ELECTRICITY.

TREAT BASE WITH TWO COATS OF A COPPER NAPHTHENATE WOOD PRESERVATIVE. SCREW ANCHORS INTO GROUND, SLOT BASE AND TIGHTEN ANCHOR TO BASE.

FRAME

USE CONSTRUCTION GRADE FIR.

PAINT FRAME WITH AN EXTERIOR WHITE PAINT. DOORS CAN BE PLACED IN ONE OR BOTH END WALLS.

COVERING

FOR YEAR AROUND USE, TWO LAYERS OF PLASTIC SHOULD BE USED.

FOR SPRING AND FALL USE, SINGLE LAYER IS SUFFICIENT.

TO REDUCE LABOR OF REPLACING PLASTIC, A 4-5 YEAR ULTRA-VIOLET RESISTANT VINYL PLASTIC SHOULD BE USED ON THE OUTSIDE.

INNER LAYER CAN BE POLYETHYLENE AND CAN BE ATTACHED WITH EITHER BATTEN STRIPS OR

3/8" STAPLES OVER HEAVY TWINE.

WALKS AND BENCHES

A CENTER WALK OF STONES OR BRICKS LAID IN SAND CAN BE ADDED AFTER THE GREENHOUSE IS BUILT.

BENCHES 30-32 INCHES HIGH AND TREATED WITH A COPPER NAPHTHENATE WOOD PRESERVATIVE CAN BE ADDED FOR CONVENIENCE.

VENTILATION

A 10 INCH DIAMETER FAN WITH AUTOMATIC LOUVER AND THERMOSTAT SHOULD BE PLACED ABOVE DOOR ON ONE END WALL.

LOCATE A 10 OR 12 INCH INTAKE LOUVER ABOVE DOOR ON OPPOSITE END WALL.

PLACE THERMOSTAT ALONG SIDEWALL NEAR PLANT LEVEL.

HEAT

HEAT MAY BE SUPPLIED FROM THE HOME HEATING SYSTEM OR FROM A SEPARATE HEATER. OUTPUT REQUIRED CAN BE OBTAINED FROM THE FOLLOW-ING TABLE.

MINIMUM OUTSIDE TEMPERATURE	SINGLE LAYER PLASTIC BTU/HR			DOUBLE LAYER PLASTIC BTU/HR		
30°	6800	10200	13600	3800	5700	7600
20°	10200	13600	17000	5700	7600	9500
10°	13600	17000	20400	7600	9500	11400
0°	17000	20400	23800	9500	11400	13300
-10°	20400	23800	27100	11400	13300	15200
	50°	60°	70°	50°	60°	70°
		MINIMUM INSIDE TEMPERATURE				

COOPERATIVE EXTENSION WORK IN
AGRICULTURE and HOME ECONOMICS
AGRICULTURAL ENGINEERING DEPARTMENT
UNIVERSITY of CONNECTICUT
STORRS, CONNECTICUT
AND
U.S. DEPARTMENT OF AGRICULTURE COOPERATING

"A" FRAME HOME GREENHOUSE

DR. BY JWB   CK. BY REP   SHEET 1 OF 2
SCALE SHOWN   DATE 7-3-67   PLAN # 238

PERSPECTIVE

DIAGONAL BRACE (1" x 3" x 12")

1" x 4" RIDGE

2'-6"   2'-6"   2'-6"   2'-6"

10'-0"

SIDE VIEW
SCALE: 1/2" = 1'-0"

SEE DOOR DETAIL

2" x 3" RAFTER

GUSSET "B"

10'-0"   10'-0"

2'-6"   1'-8"   2'-0"

6'-2"

GUSSET "A"

SEE BASE DETAIL

END VIEW
SCALE: 1/2" = 1'-0"

Plan 9(a)

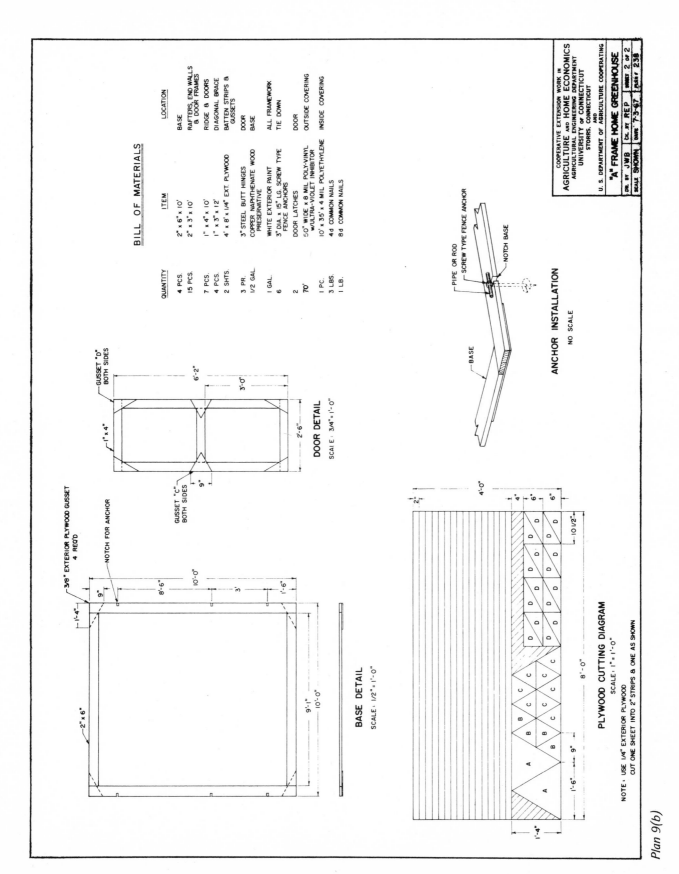

BILL OF MATERIALS

QUANTITY	ITEM	LOCATION
4 PCS.	2" x 6" x 10'	BASE
15 PCS.	2" x 3" x 10'	RAFTERS, END WALLS & DOOR FRAMES
7 PCS.	1" x 4" x 10'	RIDGE & DOORS
4 PCS.	1" x 3" x 12'	DIAGONAL BRACE
2 SHTS.	4' x 8' x 1/4" EXT. PLYWOOD	BATTEN STRIPS & GUSSETS
3 PR.	3" STEEL BUTT HINGES	DOOR
1/2 GAL.	COPPER NAPHTHENATE WOOD PRESERVATIVE	BASE
1 GAL.	WHITE EXTERIOR PAINT	ALL FRAMEWORK
6	3" DIA. x 15" LG. SCREW TYPE FENCE ANCHORS	TIE DOWN
2	DOOR LATCHES	DOOR
70'	50" WIDE x 8 MIL POLY-VINYL w/ULTRA-VIOLET INHIBITOR	OUTSIDE COVERING
1 PC.	10' x 35' x 4 MIL POLYETHYLENE	INSIDE COVERING
3 LBS.	4d COMMON NAILS	
1 LB.	8d COMMON NAILS	

DOOR DETAIL

SCALE : 3/4"=1'-0"

GUSSET "D" BOTH SIDES

1" x 4"

GUSSET "C" BOTH SIDES

6'-2"

3'-0"

2'-6"

9"

ANCHOR INSTALLATION

NO SCALE

PIPE OR ROD

SCREW TYPE FENCE ANCHOR

NOTCH BASE

BASE

BASE DETAIL

SCALE : 1/2" = 1'-0"

3/8" EXTERIOR PLYWOOD GUSSET 4 REQ'D

NOTCH FOR ANCHOR

2" x 6"

9"

8'-6"

10'-0"

3'

1'-6"

1'-4"

9'-1"

10'-0"

PLYWOOD CUTTING DIAGRAM

SCALE : 1" = 1'-0"

NOTE : USE 1/4" EXTERIOR PLYWOOD
CUT ONE SHEET INTO 2" STRIPS & ONE AS SHOWN

2"

4'-0"

4"

6"

6"

10 1/2"

8'-0"

1'-6"

9"

1'-4"

COOPERATIVE EXTENSION WORK IN
AGRICULTURE AND HOME ECONOMICS
AGRICULTURAL ENGINEERING DEPARTMENT
UNIVERSITY OF CONNECTICUT
STORRS, CONNECTICUT
AND
U. S. DEPARTMENT OF AGRICULTURE COOPERATING

"A" FRAME HOME GREENHOUSE

| DR. BY JWB | CH. BY REP | SHEET 2 OF 2 |
| SCALE SHOWN | DATE 7-3-67 | PLAN 258 |

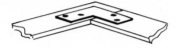

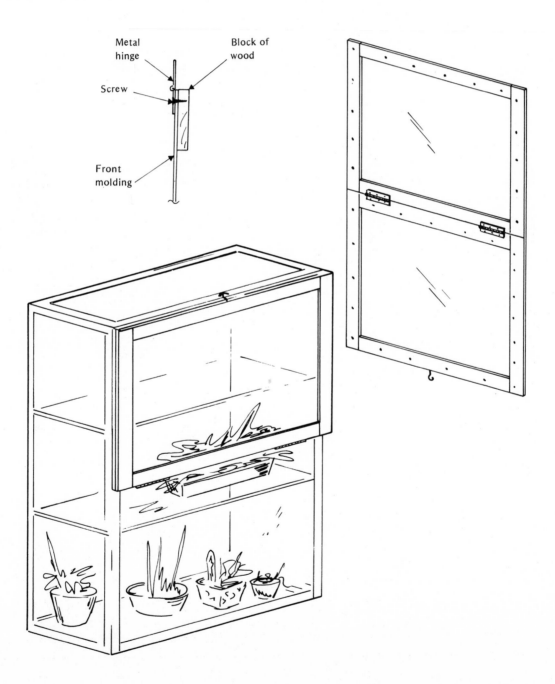

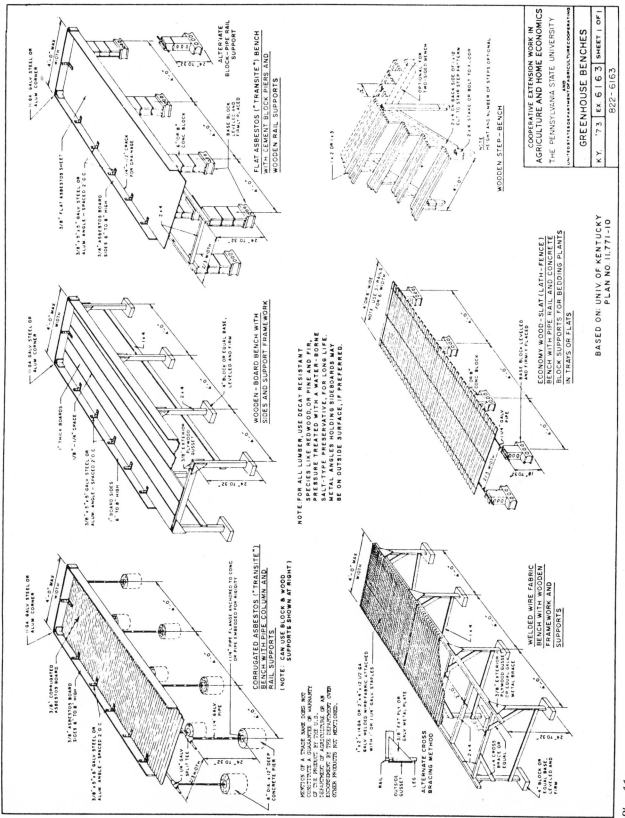

The diagram accompanying the plan for the smaller, wire-mesh hotbed gives a clear picture of how heating cables are best installed. Note that they are embedded in a layer of sand before topsoil is applied.

Greenhouse-coldframe

This is a handy hybrid—a small greenhouse that can be disassembled and used as a coldframe (see Plan 7). The hinged-roof upper section, when installed atop the lower wooden frame, allows ease of entry through its Dutch door and plenty of head-and-work room inside. When removed, it is placed at ground level to become a sloped coldframe affording easy access to plants. The roof vent can be used whether the whole unit or the coldframe alone is in service. The two sections, of course, are glazed separately with plastic film.

This is one design that makes up for its smaller size not only with its versatility but also with its complete portability.

Leanto

The leanto design is ideal for many would-be greenhouse gardeners, and this design from the University of Connecticut (Plan 8) is proportioned to complement most homes and large outbuildings. Although the basic framing materials specified are construction-grade fir lumber, the builder could substitute the higher-priced but more durable redwood. You will note that three possible coverings are suggested: single-layer polyethylene; double-layer ultraviolet-inhibitor polyethylene; or, for greatest durability, 5-ounce fiberglass.

A-Frame

This A-Frame (Plan 9) also comes from Connecticut. It is one of the simpler designs to build, and its 10' by 10' floor plan means that it can be tucked away neatly in a corner of most suburban lots. The acuteness of the floor-ground angle, however, will necessitate careful planning of the use of below-bench growing space. Select plants noted for their low growth and shade-loving tendencies.

Window greenhouse

There is a wide assortment of prefabricated aluminum-window greenhouses on the market today. Nevertheless, they are not difficult to build from plans, and the home gardener may prefer this approach as a means of custom-fitting an unusual window space. Any plan can be modified to suit individual circumstances, provided that the basic construction requisites are observed (see Plan 10).

One essential difference in the following window greenhouse design is its inward projection, rather than outward-facing profile common in these installations. This design will appeal to those who cannot construct a permanent or semipermanent addition to their window openings because of height, fire codes, landlord objections, or other reasons. Placed in a sunny window, however, this unit will accommodate far more plants than the usual windowsill arrangement—and it will look nicer too.

Windows, especially in older buildings, vary greatly in size and proportion. Therefore, this design allows for variation in length and width. The important thing to remember is that the lumber to be used is 1" by 2" throughout, and that the methods for butting the frame members are the same regardless of the length of the members themselves. Directions are thus given without reference to specific dimensions.

Geodesic

Builders interested in undertaking a geodesic greenhouse project can write to Popular Science, Plans Dept., 380 Madison Avenue, New York, N.Y. 10017, for plans for the "Sun-Dome" geodesic, which were originally published in that magazine.

Benches

As we saw earlier in this chapter, there are a number of materials and designs to use in the construction of plant benches. Here are six ideas incorporating the most common choices. All may be extended lengthwise as far as is necessary, provided the supports continue to be placed at the prescribed intervals (see Plan 11).

Chapter 4 HEATING, COOLING, VENTILATION, AND SHADE

HEATING METHODS

Heating the home greenhouse is a team effort between the gardener and the sun. As was pointed out earlier, there are a number of ways in which the gardener can make the sun's work easier—by positioning the greenhouse in a sheltered, sunny spot away from cold winds; by avoiding tall evergreens in the nearby landscape; and by insulating glass or rigid plastic structures with an inner layer of air-trapping polyurethane. During the winter, however, and on cool evenings in the fall and spring, the greenhouse owner must pick up his share of the work—this is where heating systems come into play.

Plant needs

The basic options available for heating your greenhouse are the same as those available for heating your home. The varying factors influencing the choice and application of these options, though, are perhaps even more numerous than those which face the homeowner. Prevailing climate conditions, of course, influence both. But while the home environment must always be engineered to fit human needs, the manufactured climate required by plants varies radically from species to species. Horticulturists frequently use these differing temperature requirements to establish three basic categories of greenhouse environment: cool, medium, and warm.

Temperatures in the cool greenhouse seldom exceed 50 degrees Fahrenheit (10°C) during the night, and may reach down into the mid-40's (7–8°C). Night-time temperatures in the medium range stay in the low to mid-50's (11–13°C); while warmer greenhouses will register 60 degrees Fahrenheit (16°C) during the same hours. Daytime temperatures will generally range 10 to 15 degrees Fahrenheit (5–8°C) higher. (Remember that part of this daytime increase will be provided by the sun.) Thus, the workload to be placed on the greenhouse heating system will be determined in large part by the requirements of the plants under cultivation.

Plants that prefer a cooler environment include aster, gladiolus, primrose, cyclamen, carnation, snapdragon, and daisy. Warm temperatures are best for varieties such as philodendron, rose, begonia, African violet, hyacinth, lily, coleus, and daffodil, with some tropical foliage preferring a night-time temperature of as high as 75 degrees Fahrenheit (25°C). The middle range is a favorable one for a long list of popular flowering or foliage plants, with many strains of varieties generally associated with the warm or cool extremes also doing well at these compromise temperatures. Here the gardener will learn a great deal through experimentation.

Although it is a good idea to select the temperature range to be maintained and choose plants accordingly (or vice versa, unless the warmth-loving tropicals would put too great a strain on the heating budget), most greenhouses will surprise their owners by harboring varying temperature zones in certain corners or out-of-the-way spots. These are evidence of the peculiarities of air currents carrying heat from its sources, and of the inevitable rising of hot air; these zones can be located by placing thermometers at intervals throughout the enclosure. Take advantage of such warmer and cooler spots by using them to grow plants that might not fit in with the prevailing temperatures in the greenhouse (see chart in Appendix B).

The other major factors influencing greenhouse heating are the nature and size of the new installation. A very small greenhouse, especially one in a mild climate, might be satisfactorily served by a space heater—more

The Wandering Jew growing underneath the bench at left does well in a warm greenhouse. The terrarium cacti, right, enjoy relatively low humidity as well as a medium-warm environment.

about these later. Should the greenhouse be an attached model, one of the first possibilities that will occur to the builder will be that of enlisting his home heating plant to take on the new chores. This is a frequently employed solution, and one which can even be made to work with a free-standing greenhouse, provided it is reasonably close to the home. Applications may vary from simply leaving open the door to a small leanto, to extending steam or hot-water pipes underground to an adjoining or nearby structure. Remember, though, that any greenhouse larger than a window model will place increased demands on the home heating plant. Anyone considering this alternative should consult a heating specialist. He'll let you know whether your present installation, i.e., furnace, boiler, etc., will be able to take on the extra work without major alterations; or, if not, what these alterations should include.

Your home heating system is not the only thing you might eventually wish to expand. Remember that your greenhouse may grow along with the plants in it—a good reason for starting off with a more-than-adequate heat source.

Fuels

Most homeowners are aware of the basic choices in fuels and heat-conducting systems. Let's look first at the leading fuels: coal, oil, gas, and electricity.

Coal, once a near-universal fuel for greenhouse furnaces as well as those in homes, may now be virtually dismissed unless the gardener lives near inexpensive supplies of low-sulphur coal which can be delivered regularly. The soot generated by the soft coals is quite properly regarded as incompatible with the delicate environment the greenhouse seeks to encourage; and the finer grades are not always easy to obtain.

What about oil? Of course, the price of heating oil —and that of all other sources of energy—has risen dramatically in recent years. No homeowner needs to be reminded of that. But remember that you will be heating a greenhouse, not another home; and that the glass or plastic-covered structure is one utilizer of a "solar heating" system under development for use in the near future. Oil has the advantage of availability, cleanliness, and adaptability to hot water, steam, or hot air systems.

These virtues are shared by natural gas, whether received via city lines or supplied in bottled form. Gas

This Lord and Burnham "Holiday" gas-fired hot water boiler fits compactly in a corner of the greenhouse.

heat is considered much safer for use in greenhouses now that burners have been developed which effectively seal off fumes from inside, where they pose a danger to plants (and to gardeners, should ventilation be less than sufficient).

Electricity runs the risk of being the most expensive source of heat, except in select areas (usually near hydro projects) where rates are significantly lower. However, this does not detract from electricity's usefulness in space-heating devices, or in soil-heating cables and infrared lights. None of this apparatus can be used exclusively to heat a large greenhouse, and even smaller units (hotbeds excepted) cannot adequately served by "lights" or cables alone.

Equipment

In addition to the choice of fuel, the greenhouse gardener must decide how the heat is to be delivered. The three standard alternatives are steam, hot water, and hot air.

Steam seems to have slipped in popularity as a vehicle for greenhouse heat, although many of the large com-

mercial establishments continue to depend upon it. Part of the reason for its decline among amateurs is its concurrent disappearance in homes; it is unlikely that a gardener will install a steam system where one does not already exist. Perhaps another drawback is the relative difficulty of adding another zone to a steam system, in the event of further greenhouse expansion. Even initial installation of steam heat is a job for a professional.

One of the advantages of steam is its secondary capacity as a soil-sterilizing agent. This is a technique long used by professionals, and one that might appeal to the organic gardener, whose soil pest-control measures must be limited to nonchemical means. Certain new hot-water boilers, however, now incorporate an auxiliary steam reserve to be tapped for exactly this purpose.

Hot-water heat has clearly taken the lead in all but the smallest home greenhouses. The prevalence of hot-water systems in homes has led many gardeners to divert heat from the larger building to the smaller via a gravity system or circulating pump; some of the larger greenhouse manufacturers even supply kits to accomplish this expansion with a minimum of expense.

The compact size of many of the newer oil or gas-fired hot water units, meanwhile, has made them a practical, moderately priced installation for free-standing greenhouses. Another advantage of hot water over steam is its fuel economy during marginally cold weather. In spring and fall, or during southern winters, a lower intensity of furnace heat is required to maintain a desirable temperature. Steam heat does not function until the water in the system boils and the steam circulates through the pipes. Hot water, however, may be heated to moderate temperatures, yet still produce the required effect.

There are various ways of installing such a hot-water system. The conventional approach, which is quite effective in a permanent structure with a full foundation, is to house the burner/boiler either in an enclosed workroom at one end of the greenhouse, or, if it is a compact model, out of the way beneath a bench. The pipes extending from the boiler—or from the basement of a nearby or adjoining dwelling—are arranged along the perimeter of the foundation in rows. As many as four or five rows of standard 2-inch iron pipe may be used or fewer if the pipes are equipped with heat-radiating fins. These fins (identical to those used in home hot-water heating) greatly increase the radiating surface of the pipe. This serves to boost the efficiency of the system and saves fuel costs.

One of the more promising improvements in hot-water heat delivery is the overhead unit, which is an ideal source of heat in greenhouses where space is at a pre-

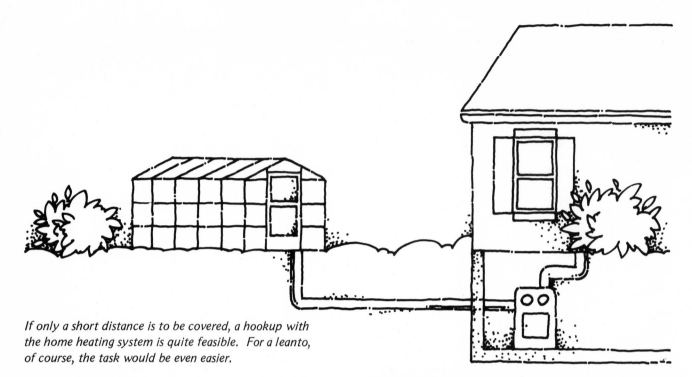

If only a short distance is to be covered, a hookup with the home heating system is quite feasible. For a leanto, of course, the task would be even easier.

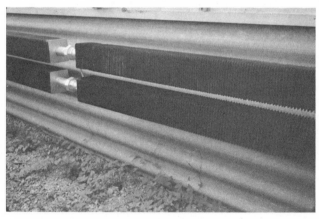

Finned hot water pipes increase heating efficiency.

This oil-fired hot water heater is installed horizontally along the greenhouse floor. (Courtesy Lord & Burnham)

mium. Water heated in such a unit in turn heats air, which is circulated throughout the area in a diffuse fashion designed to eliminate hot blasts directed at any plant-growing areas.

Hot air was long thought to be a poor source of heat for greenhouses because of its tendency to dry the indoor environment—a decided disadvantage in a greenhouse, where sustained moisture is vital. But the ease and inex-

pensiveness with which such systems can be installed, either separately or as a continuation of home heating, has led gardeners to seek ways of overcoming the dryness factor.

In all but the least sophisticated hot-air heated greenhouses, a humidifier is the obvious answer. Humidifiers either can be separate portable units, or may be installed in conjunction with the heat source itself, as they frequently are in homes. In either case, it is a good idea to regulate them automatically by means of a humidistat, which does for humidity control what a thermostat does for temperature: it activates the humidifier when it senses

These overhead-mounted hot water heaters take up no valuable work space, yet are engineered to dispense heat evenly throughout the greenhouse. At left, a horizontally-mounted model; at right, a vertical-delivery type. (Courtesy Modine Co.)

Cool is the right word for these young cukes, growing in a well-humidified section of a summer greenhouse.

Two examples of greenhouse humidifiers. The simple, highly portable model at the top is ideal for a small greenhouse, or one whose moisture requirements are small; a larger and more powerful unit (bottom) can still be tucked neatly under a bench. (Courtesy Lord & Burnham)

A greenhouse waterfall can serve many purposes—not the least of which is purely esthetic. Just as important, they humidify the area around them and serve as a gathering spot for moisture-loving plants. This one is in the University of Vermont greenhouse, but smaller models can be installed in home units.

an insufficiency of moisture in the air, and shuts it off when the proper balance has been attained.

Although the automatic humidifier is not a terribly expensive addition to a greenhouse heating installation, owners of smaller leantos and space-heated free-standing models might simply wish to place a pan of water near the hot-air outlet. Evaporation will take care of the rest.

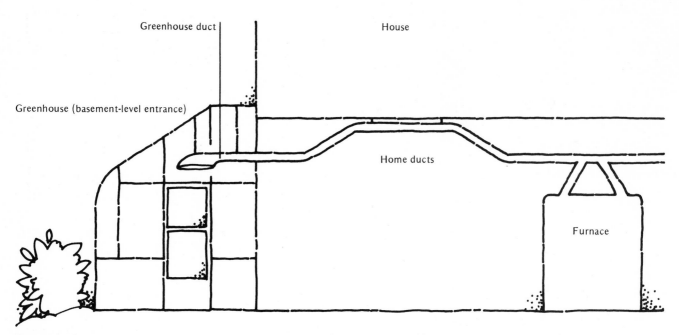

Diagram of air duct installation.

An innovative approach used by some gardeners with the room to spare is a small, pump-activated ornamental waterfall, which likewise humidifies by evaporation. There is a pleasant corner of the Botany Department greenhouse at the University of Vermont in which such a water fall spills into a small trough stocked with goldfish. The steady patter of the water and rippling motion of the fish complement the colors and smells of the flowers and make this greenhouse seem quite another world.

Another humidification device is installed as a part of the cooling and ventilation system, and consists of a pad of moistened material aligned at a vent opposite the ventilator fan in an even-span house. As the fan draws air through this vent, it carries water vapor along with it. We'll take a closer look at this arrangement later on.

Aside from these simple answers to the humidity question, there are other features of hot-air heat that make it an attractive alternative. It is by far the easiest permanent system to install, requiring none of the precision fitting or "sweating" of pipes necessary in the construction of a steam or hot-water system. The hot air is carried to where it is needed via aluminum or galvanized ducts or a plastic tube system. A similar duct operates in conjunction with a fan to draw in air to be reheated and recirculated. These ducts can be installed by a competent amateur, and can extend either from a heater installed in the greenhouse, or from the main unit in the home. Don't overextend the ducts; significant heat loss can result if the hot air is forced to travel too great a distance from source

A compact space heater can be a big help on extra-cold nights, or as a standby unit. Be sure to choose one that will distribute heat evenly. (Courtesy Lord & Burnham)

to outlet—especially if this route passes through unheated or underheated space outside the greenhouse.

Very small greenhouses heated by hot air may need no ducts; the air will enter the room directly from the heater face. However, it is very important in such circumstances to see to it that the hot air is deflected from direct contact with nearby plants. Fans help control this, and also help circulate heat freely through the greenhouse.

There are many different types of space heaters; their use in the indoor garden ranges from that of auxiliary equipment on bitter nights, to emergency insurance, to complete heating systems for small or temporary structures. Gardeners intending to use them should keep two things in mind: they should not be relied upon to perform

This compact gas heater will release no dangerous fumes into the greenhouse. (Courtesy Lord & Burnham)

These soil heating cables and their accompanying thermostat improve growing conditions for young seedlings.

tasks for which they are not designed; and, their operators should be thoroughly familiar with their safe use.

One of the simplest space heaters is the radiant electric model often used for auxiliary heat in homes. It is a poor choice as a heater for the home greenhouse, or even as a secondary source in a larger one. The reason lies in its very simplicity: the heat emanating from the glowing coils in these units travels in only one direction, and this spells trouble for any plants in its path. Also, the air in other parts of the greenhouse will not become appreciably warmer.

More sophisticated electric heaters, equipped with thermostatic controls and air-circulation fans, will prove far more satisfactory. These are usually available in 1- to 4-kilowatt sizes to be connected directly to the home fusebox via a 220-volt circuit, and are often used successfully in pairs or even in multiple numbers, in large greenhouses in moderate climates. For reasons of economy, their use is discouraged in structures intended to be kept in the "warm" range outlined above, or in extremely cold locations. In installing these electric heaters, the gardener should take the same advice as that which would apply to an expansion of home heating systems: See to it that the existing facilities are up to the new demands being placed upon them. This means having an electrician check the capacity of fuseboxes, circuit breakers, and wiring.

Gas is an efficient fuel for space heaters although, for reasons of safety, such devices must be more permanently mounted in order for fumes to be dealt with properly. A compact solution now offered by some manufacturers is for the small gas space heater to be installed in a foundation wall, with the combustion taking place in a chamber sealed off from the inside and vented outdoors. Once again, these units must be fitted with a fan to distribute the heat evenly.

Any heater intended for standby use will be worthless if it is connected to the same source of supply as the main system. If a power failure might be the cause of heat shutoff, then the auxiliary system must be nonelectric. The exception would be in the case of greenhouses large enough, or of plant collections delicate and valuable enough, to warrant a gasoline-powered electric generator, such as those manufactured by Kohler and McCulloch. Few home gardeners will care to go this route.

In an emergency, catalytic heaters of the type often used for family camping will provide needed greenhouse heat. Just remember that all combustion consumes oxygen, and that some ventilation must therefore be provided. Remember also that most nontropical plant varieties will be able to withstand a brief temperature drop without any marked damage.

One precaution frequently recommended by greenhouse experts is an alarm system, which can be activated by any undesired indoor climatic change, whether it be caused by lack of heat, dryness, or failure of ventilators to function. The National Greenhouse Company is one supplier of these devices.

As we saw before, soil-heating cables must definitely be relegated to the status of auxiliary heating equipment, although within their range of use, as in hotbeds, they can be most effective for propagating seedlings. The best procedure for their installation is that outlined in the diagram accompanying the USDA hotbed plans referenced in the preceding chapter. The layer of sand in which the cables are embedded should be kept damp, since dry sand is a less effective heat conductor. Under no circumstances should the cables be placed in peat. As

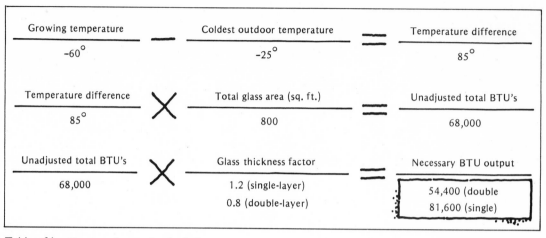

Table of heating requirement calculations.

peat dries, it will insulate the cable more and more, eventually causing overheating.

Where soil-heating cables are to be used outdoors, in hotbeds, a level of 10 to 15 watts of heat per square foot should be provided. In the greenhouse, where the main heating system does the bulk of the work, a less intensive application of the cable is acceptable.

CALCULATING HEATING REQUIREMENTS

Regardless of fuels and conducting agents, basic requirements exist for the amount of energy needed to heat a given enclosure to a given temperature. These requirements are stated in British Thermal Units, or BTU's. A calculation of anticipated necessary heat output, in terms of BTU's per hour, will help the prospective greenhouse owner decide which fuel is most economical to use, and may even assist in a decision concerning the size of the structure and the types of plants to be grown.

The following method for calculating BTU requirements has been recommended by the U.S. Department of Agriculture. It is a simple one for the home gardener to use. The final figures arrived at will represent the necessary hourly output, in BTU's, of the greenhouse heating system.

First, calculate the difference between the temperature at which you expect to grow plants, and the coldest anticipated night-time outdoor temperature in your area. A New England gardner might experience an occasional winter low of -25 degrees, while he would prefer the inside of his greenhouse to maintain 60 degrees at night. The difference, therefore, is 85 degrees.

Next, multiply this figure by the *total exposed square footage* of glass or plastic on your greenhouse.

Don't forget sides and ends. If the total glass area measures, say, 800 square feet, multiply it by the temperature differential (in this case 85), and arrive at the figure of 68,000.

Finally, adjust this figure according to the thickness of the greenhouse roof and walls. If they are of double-layer plastic or glass lined with plastic, multiply by 0.8; for single-layer coverings, multiply by 1.2.

Here are the figures for our hypothetical New England greenhouse:

—For a double-layer structure (68,000 x 0.8): 54,400 BTU's per hour.

—For a single-layer structure (68,000 x 1.2): 81,600 BTU's per hour.

Now you are ready to advise your heating specialist of the required output of the system to be installed, and it can be planned accordingly. (Remember that a 10 percent margin is desirable.) You are also in a position to estimate fuel costs, given the units of each fuel (gallons of oil, cubic feet of natural gas, kilowatt-hours of electricity) needed to produce x-amount of BTU's. These figures, as well as the cost per unit, are available from local utilities and fuel dealers.

SUMMER COOLING

Just as the gardener must see to it that temperatures in the greenhouse do not drop too low during the winter, he must also make sure that excessive heat does not injure the plants during warm weather. This precaution is especially important where plants are expected to flower. We are not concerned here with the use of a conventional home-type air conditioner, which would be expensive to

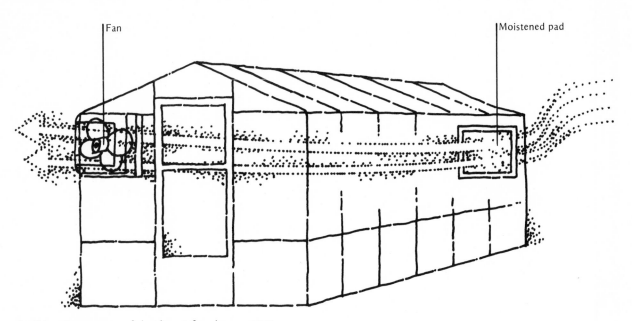

Fan

Moistened pad

In this setup, a powerful exhaust fan draws water through a perpetually moistened pad in order to cool greenhouse interior.

run and is not really suited to the maintenance of a growing environment. Rather, greenhouse cooling incorporates simpler methods, which are used in conjunction with ventilation systems.

Moistened pad system

In looking at ways to solve the humidification problem, we saw that air drawn into the greenhouse through a moistened pad helps alleviate the drying effects of some forms of artificial heat. This procedure will also lower temperatures inside the greenhouse—sometimes as much as 40 degrees, depending on outdoor heat and dryness. (In excessively arid areas, indoor temperature reduction will be most dramatic.)

During the operation of this type of cooler, all vents and louvres other than those aligned with the pad are closed. This pad is generally filled with aspen fiber; no substance has been found which exceeds aspen in moisture retention. Water is continually dripped through this spongy material (a small recirculating pump is included with most commercially available systems), and enters the greenhouse environment as a cooling vapor.

Some self-contained systems feature an intake fan in the same unit as the pad; here hot outside air comes directly into contact with the water and enters the greenhouse already cooled. This will necessitate some open ventilators or exhaust fans elsewhere in the structure.

A self-contained unit such as this will deliver cool, moistened air to greenhouse plants during periods of dry, hot weather. (Courtesy Lord & Burnham)

As with heat, there are formulas for estimating cooling requirements, should you feel that this "evaporative" cooling system is a requisite for your climate or plant collection. Here is a simple guideline from the U.S. De-

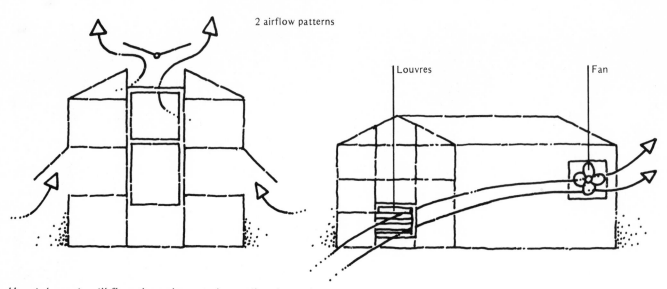

2 airflow patterns

Louvres

Fan

Here is how air will flow through properly ventilated greenhouses.

partment of Agriculture: Calculate the total volume of your greenhouse (width x length x average height); then multiply this figure by 11/2. This represents the cubic feet per minute (CFM) air-capacity rating you should look for in a self-contained commercial unit.

Should you choose the pad-opposite-fan system, select a fan that will exceed the drawing capacity necessary for simple air circulation. In installing the pad, remember that one square foot of this material, moistened with 1/3 gallon of water per minute, will cool approximately 140 cubic feet of air in the same amount of time.

Don't forget that any open access to the greenhouse, even by way of wet, close-packed fibers, is an invitation to pests. Obviously only the tiniest insects will be able to pass through the cooling pad, but to ensure against their entry, add dieldrin (1 cup per 25 gallons of circulating water) to the system. Gardeners intending to use a self-contained system must keep in mind that for effective cooling, the unit must be installed *outside* the greenhouse, with a short duct transmitting cooled air inside. Coolers set up indoors will humidifiy, but will not actually cool.

The pad-opposite-fan system is in common use in large greenhouses, while the self-contained models are popular with owners of smaller installations.

VENTILATION

Temperature and humidity are two important factors in the greenhouse environment. Another is proper ventilation. Apparatus for ensuring air circulation ranges from

the hinged top panel of a window greenhouse to the automated series of louvres and movable sashes found in big even-spans. Each of these devices performs the vital task of moving stale air away from plants and allowing fresh air in.

In addition to containing the carbon dioxide that plants need to grow, a fresh air flow also inhibits disease, and makes temperature regulation easier in warm weather. This last benefit is particularly important in the small greenhouse, where summer heat can become intolerable to plants (and to anyone working with them) in no time at all.

Hot air rises, as everyone knows; for this reason greenhouse vents are best place nearer the roof line. The shape which they take will largely depend upon the design of the building. Those in a geodesic dome, for instance, will consist of one or more of the triangular panels hinged so that it may be propped open. The more conventional designs tend towards the use of ridge vents and/or gable-end fans and louvres. The ridge vents are particularly useful in an even-span house erected perpendicular to prevailing winds (remember that in North America these are usually westerlies; the well-placed even-span will have a gable end facing north). A leanto had best not face its sole ridge vent towards the prevailing winds, however, since this opening would provide a ready and inflexible access for winter winds.

The ridge vent, as incorporated into the design of many prefabricated greenhouses, particularly the aluminum models, is simply a movable section of sash near the peak of the roof, running parallel to the roof line itself. It is designed to be lifted by an attached bar or, in heavier

Ridge vent in open position on leanto greenhouse.

Devices such as these automatically raise and lower ridge vents. (Courtesy J. A. Nearing Co.)

This small greenhouse makes use of a fan-louvre combination, in which the exhaust fan mounted at the far end draws air through the open glass louvres beside the door. (Courtesy Lord & Burnham)

Side and gable vents

Vents in the side walls of greenhouses are usually hinged at the top, moved outward at the bottom, and propped open. When used in conjunction with ridge vents, they allow a continuous updraft and expulsion of warmed air.

A continuous passage of air lengthwise through the greenhouse is assured by the installation of a vent-and-fan system at the gable ends. This is especially suitable in designs such as the Quonset or Gothic arch which cannot be readily adapted to ridge vents. In an even-span attached at one gable end to a home, this ventilation might be accomplished by installing an exhaust fan at the outside gable, and leaving open the door to the house.

The exhaust fan is frequently used in conjunction with a louvred vent, which can be opened or closed depending upon whether the fan is in operation. In simple installations, light louvres will open to admit air as the fan creates a vacuum against them; more complex arrangements are available in which both fan and louvres are activated by a thermostat. It's a good idea to install thermostatic fan controls even in a small greenhouse where the louvres are not to be opened by the same method. Rising and falling outside temperatures are the best index of the need for fresh air, and the gardener is not always nearby to watch his thermometers and flip the fan switch accordingly.

versions, a geared apparatus operated by a pulley. These installations may be activated by thermostatic controls which determine the need for ventilation on the basis of rising temperatures within the greenhouse. Serious greenhousepeople praise these devices for the precision with which they regulate air flow and prevent heat loss; it is up to the amateur to weigh their moderate cost against the attention required for manual operation.

A variation on the automated ridge vent, useful in areas prone to electrical failure, employs gas-filled cylinders which lift panels hydraulically when heat expands their contents.

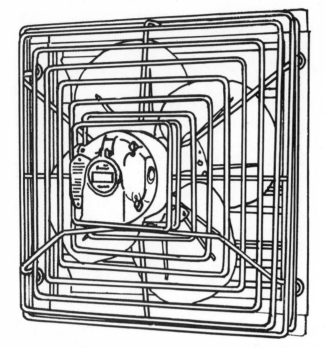

A greenhouse exhaust fan. (Courtesy J. A. Nearing Co.)

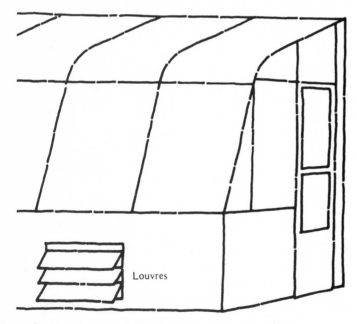

Louvres

Position for foundation louvre.

Selecting and installing the fan

How powerful a fan will you need? A simple rule of thumb states that the greenhouse should receive a complete change of air every minute. Exhaust fans are sold with a volume-per-minute rating, based upon their ca-

pacity at ⅛-inch static pressure. The volume in this figure, of course, should equal that of the greenhouse. A two-speed fan will allow greater ventilation flexibility in a medium-sized or large space.

Remember where the warmest air tends to go, and install the fan as high in the wall as possible. This will also reduce drafts on plants. A more thorough circulation is sometimes accomplished by placing jalousie vents or louvres low on side on opposite walls, either set into a high foundation or in place of a low window light. If you expect the fan to pull air through movable louvres at a distance of several yards, the building must be tightly constructed.

Convection Tube

Another ventilation system couples the fan with a tubular plastic duct that runs the length of the roof line. Air drawn into this suspended duct is distributed gently into the greenhouse via small openings along the duct's surface. This is called "convection tube" ventilation. As with other efficient air-circulation systems, it has the effect of lowering summer temperatures as well as providing needed carbon dioxide and oxygen.

Wherever possible, vent openings should be screened. This will keep out pests as well as discourage bees. Although bees are rightfully thought of as the gardener's friends, they can be a nuisance in places where flowers are expected to bloom over a prolonged period, as pollination causes quicker bloom fade. Birds, too, will occasionally be attracted to the unscreened greenhouse.

Some flexible form of screening, perhaps plastic, will be needed where hinged vents that open outward are in use.

Air circulation

Aside from actual ventilation—bringing in outside air—greenhouse gardeners are often concerned with the circulation of air within the enclosure during times when vents to the outside are closed. In small greenhouses, this problem can be solved by bringing in an electric desk fan —just be sure it does not blow directly on any of the plants.

SHADING

Shading is another important means of keeping greenhouse temperatures down during the "dog days." Well-placed shades will not inhibit growth, since the brightest

A household fan is often sufficient for circulating air in the small greenhouse.

The roller shades on this even-span are fully extended; except where extremely sensitive plants are being cultivated, this should be necessary only on the hottest days. (Courtesy Lord & Burnham)

summer days usually provide much more light than plants need.

How to provide shade? We know that stragetically located hardwood trees will do the job, without keeping out winter light. But few gardeners can count on large trees being situated exactly where they are needed, and they take an awfully long time to grow. Clearly, some artificial shading is required.

Manufacturers of prefabricated greenhouses have met this challenge in a variety of ways, such as the A-frame with shading "wings" that project away from its sloping side walls. Other suppliers propose different solutions. Basically, these reflect the same choices available to the do-it yourselfer. Rigid and folding shades are available and even shading that can be painted on.

Rigid shading materials include wooden and aluminum slats, and fiberglass panels. The slat shades are designed to break up the direct rays of the sun into a latticed shadow. They may be homemade from fir lath, or purchased in kit form from greenhouse equipment suppliers. These commercial shades will most likely be constructed of long-lasting aluminum or redwood. Rigid shading panels allow the advantage of selective application; they can be installed over an area of the greenhouse housing shade-loving plants, while sunlight is unimpaired in other sections. One disadvantage is their relatively seasonal permanence; once installed, the gardener will probably leave them in place until fall. Thus no allowance is made for overcast days in summer.

Tinted fiberglass panels, similar to the clear ones used in greenhouse glazing, are another means of providing shade. Unlike the rigid aluminum and wooden slat shades, these are available in curved sections to fit similarly shaped eaves. One prefab manufacturer supplies them in two different tints, each allowing a different degree of light transmission. These come equipped with clips for installation, and are cut to fit the firm's various greenhouse models—a distinct advantage to those who have purchased these units.

Yet another supplier offers rolls of green-tinted plastic film, which can be cut to fit the panels to which it is to be applied. Some light films can be applied to the inside of glass panels using only water as a binder.

Tinted polyethylene sheeting hung on the inside of greenhouse walls will cut excessive summer light.

Roll shades

Perhaps the most popular greenhouse shades are the roll-up type. These are particularly compatible with lean-tos. They can be adjusted to different heights—much the same as blinds in a house window—without any climbing and dismantling. For this reason their owners are much more likely to employ them in close response to the weather.

The best rolling shades are made of thin redwood slats. They are available either in their natural tone or painted; the silvery paint usually used is designed to reflect the sun's heat. Also included are the necessary hardware and cords for installation and operation.

Bamboo shades are an inexpensive substitute for redwood blinds. They will do the job, although they are essentially made for indoor use and cannot be expected to hold up long outside. Other inexpensive and temporary outdoor shading can be devised using various nettings and loose-woven cloths.

Indoor shading

Although most greenhouse shades are designed for application on the outer surface, there are a number of ways in which shading can be accomplished indoors. Any of the nettings might be useful, provided they are held up in such a way as not to interfere with plants. Polyethylene sheeting is also a possibility. If you have been using clear polyethylene as insulation against your regular glazing during the winter, simply replace it with a tinted variety. Experiment with swatches of different shades in a corner of the greenhouse until you have decided which one will let in the amount of light you want.

Paint-on shading

An entirely different approach to shading involves the use of special paints. These are usually purchased in powder or paste form and mixed with either water or a petroleum derivative, according to the product directions. Owners of aluminum greenhouses should be careful to choose only shading compounds that are designed explicitly for use near that metal, since other products might contain corrosive lime.

Shading compounds are applied by brush, roller, or sprayer, and can be removed easily—perhaps too easily, since heavy rains can make short work of the water-based solutions. Like the rigid panels, liquid coatings can be applied selectively over certain sections of the greenhouse. Should the gardener later opt for clear glass where the compound has been applied, he may scrape or scrub it away where desired.

Synthetic lights might be subject to damage from shading products mixed with petroleum derivatives such as benzine. Ask your supplier if these compounds may be safely applied to such surfaces.

The lights of this glass greenhouse have been splashed with a shading compound. Later, it can be scraped off in strips for a less thorough shading effect.

Chapter 5 AUXILIARY EQUIPMENT AND GENERAL MAINTENANCE

WATERING AND MISTING

Along with the proper ambient temperature and humidity, regular watering is one of the most important requirements for plants. Anyone at all familiar with gardening or keeping houseplants is aware of the dangers of either infrequent or over-watering, and has no doubt learned of the special needs of his particular favorite plants. The greenhouse environment, however, creates a different set of circumstances which affects both the frequency of watering and the methods used. Specialized hardware may also be involved.

There are two things to remember when watering greenhouse plants. The first is that, unlike outdoor garden plants, your indoor plants are growing in a limited amount of soil. The second is that despite the greenhouse's near-constant exposure to the sun, it is basically an enclosed environment in which moisture is more likely to be retained than dissipated quickly—unless, of course, proper humidification is not provided during the heating season.

With these two factors in mind, we see that over-watering can be a problem in the greenhouse. In order to avoid it, the indoor gardener must learn when and how to water, and how much water to give.

An excess of water can be responsible for a number of plant maladies, some of which strike below the soil surface, and some above. A too thorough and repeated compacting of wet soil around the roots of a plant cuts off oxygen; lingering moisture on leaves is an invitation to fungus diseases. Because of this latter danger, it is always wise to water early in the day, when there will be plenty of time left for droplets on leaves to evaporate through ventilation and the effects of sunshine. Save evening watering only for emergencies, when for some rea-

son a plant or group of plants has dried during the day to the point of wilting. This is an especially important precaution with just-sprouting or very young plants still in seed flats, as they are particularly prone to overwatering damage. Remember also that water will disappear faster from plant surfaces when the air is dry—such as on cold, crisp winter days when a good deal of the moisture in a greenhouse will be drawn to inside glass walls by the lower temperatures outside.

SOME BASIC WATERING ADVICE

The best rule for watering is a simple one, and it supercedes any strict watering "schedule" the gardener might

This gardener is watering her plants with a rigid extension attached to the hose.

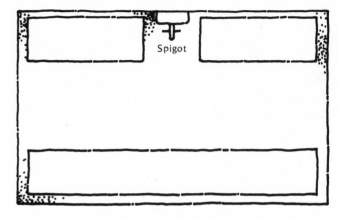

Overhead view

Whenever possible, water spigot should be given a central location.

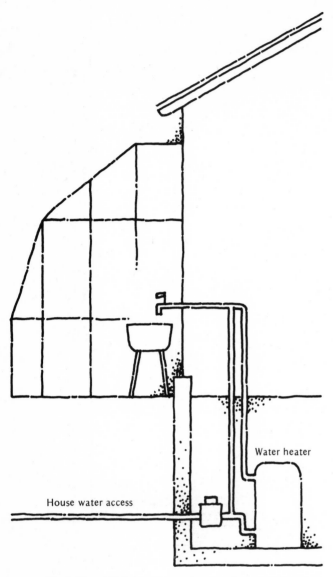

Illustration showing home-greenhouse water connections

Diagram of how water can be brought into greenhouse from basement of home.

like to impose: Water when the plants need it. The best indicator, of course, is the soil. As long as soil in pots or plant beds shows some signs of moisture, watering can wait. When you do water, however, the soil in the beds or pots should be soaked down to the bottom, as this encourages the growth of healthy and extensive root systems.

One rule of watering frequently overlooked, much to the detriment of plants, concerns the temperature of the water used. Plants do not like ice-cold water. In fact, they prefer water temperature to be within 10 degrees Fahrenheit of the temperature of the air that surrounds

them. This can pose a slight problem to the gardener who does not have a temperature regulator on his faucet, or access to a hot-water supply in his greenhouse. The solution depends on the size and location of the structure. Obviously, a large free-standing greenhouse situated at some distance from the main building should either have its own hot-water facilities or have water piped to it (pipes buried below the frostline, and over not too great a distance) from the home. Smaller free-standing units can be served by garden hose in warmer months, and by water carried in buckets or watering cans during the winter.

The leanto and other attached greenhouses have easier access to water. Permanent pipes can be passed through the home foundation into the new structure, or a hose may simply be run from a sink or other water outlet in the basement or first floor. In any event, remember that even home tap water can be nearly ice-cold in winter, and should either be mixed with warm water or allowed to stand at room temperature until it is safe for plants.

Hoses, attachments, and watering cans

If a spigot for a hose is to be installed inside a greenhouse, try to place it near the center of the building. This will cut by half the length of the hose you will need, making storage and handling easier.

The business end of the hose should also be specifically adapted for greenhouse use. As with outdoor gardens and potted houseplants, it is unwise to direct a narrow, intense stream of water at a particular spot. This causes a number of problems, among them compacting of soil and washing away of soil from around roots. Instead of using a conventional garden-spray attachment, which will either intensify the stream or diffuse it too greatly, greenhouse gardeners should fit hose ends with a "breaker" device that will lessen the force of the water stream while still allowing it to be directed where needed. One such device, the fogg-it nozzle, may be used as both a breaker and mister. These attachments are generally used in tandem with a stiff metal wand, which allows greater control of the hose and an easier reach to out-of-the-way places (well-designed bench layouts, though, should have few of these).

The old-fashioned watering can is by no means outmoded, although handy when only a small area is to

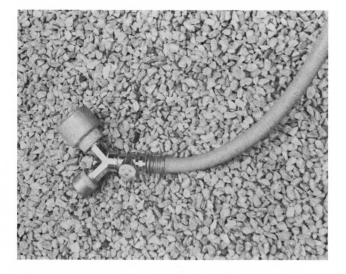

A flip of a switch changes this breaker nozzle into a mister.

be watered, or where the greenhouse is small or too far away from hose hookups. Again, the best cans for greenhouse use are those with a long spout and a handle providing easy leverage. Sprinkling nozzles, or "roses," are available for cans in varying gauges. Like the breaker nozzles on hoses, they reduce the impact of water on plants and soil.

Automated watering systems

There are a number of more elaborate watering devices designed to free the gardener from routine, and to take the guesswork out of the "when to water?" question. Some are designed for plants growing together in bench trays, and involve a plastic tube that extends along the bench. The tube sends water along a series of side nozzles directed at the soil. The frequency and duration of watering can be controlled by a master time clock; otherwise the gardener can operate the system manually simply by turning on the main hose and watching for soil saturation.

Other watering systems are used where plants are cultivated in individual pots. These use a centrally placed hose or plastic tube, from which extend a number of thin, flexible tubes fitted with weighted nozzles. Water passes directly into each pot through these nozzles. Here also the system is controlled automatically; it is mandatory, however, to limit its use only where all pots are the same size. Both of these systems—the bench type and the centrally placed tube—must be employed among plants having similar watering requirements.

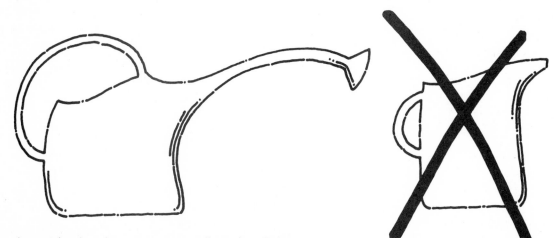

A specialized garden watering can will get the job done easily, as it can reach into out-of-the way places while still affording good leverage. A simple jug or pitcher won't do.

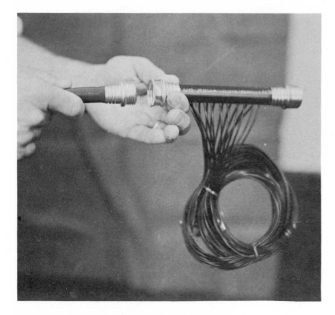

At left, the feeder pipe through which water passes on its way to tiny individual hoses in this fully automatic watering system. Photo at right shows weighted nozzle in place in flowerpot.

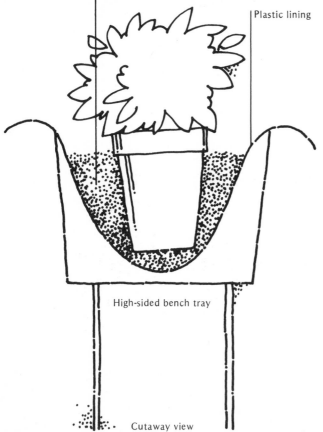

Saturated vermiculite, contained in a plastic-lined greenhouse bench tray, will provide water for plants bedded in it while gardener is away.

If an occasional vacation or weekend away is your concern, and no one is available to keep an eye on the greenhouse, a simple arrangement for "automatic watering" can be set up by placing clay pots in a deep, plastic-lined tray filled with saturated vermiculite. The water suspended in the vermiculite will be gradually absorbed by the pots, and subsequently by the soil and root structures within them.

Misting

Misting is more properly considered a means of humidification rather than watering. But since the level of humidity directly affects watering requirements, and since the hardware for installation of a misting system is similar to that used in watering, we'll take a look here at how and why it is done.

Misting is especially useful as a means of providing moisture for delicate cuttings rooting in sand, and as an auxiliary system to be used along with regular watering in providing the humid environment favored by orchids and other tropical plants.

Like watering, misting can be accomplished with either permanent or portable equipment, which can be operated either automatically or manually. The key to good results is a nozzle that produces a fine aerated stream of water, much like that from a steam iron or spray can. These nozzles are placed either at intervals on overhead pipes or tubing, or in place of regular attachments on garden hoses. The idea is to create a mist of fast-evaporating droplets, which will moisten plants gently while humidifying the air.

The misting nozzle provides a fine spray for plants.

Gardeners wishing to use misting only as a source of occasional added moisture would do best to buy a simple hose misting nozzle, frequently available for less than a dollar.

THERMOSTATS, TIMERS, AND OTHER AUTOMATIC CONTROLS

Mention of the various automatic control devices used for regulation of watering and misting systems, as well as those used to help run heaters, ventilators, and coolers, might frighten the prospective greenhouse builder into thinking that the indoor garden is a robotized display of technology rather than of plants. This is hardly the case, and can be easily avoided. First, although each of the automatically controlled operations described has its place in amateur greenhouse gardening, it is unlikely that any single, small- to moderate-sized installation will incorporate all of them. A small northern greenhouse, for instance, might be so situated and ventilated as to need no artificial cooling system. Or a gardener may prefer to do his watering and vent operation by hand. Humidifiers and humidistats are an absolute necessity only when the gardener suspects that climatic conditions or artificial heating will create an overly dry atmosphere in the greenhouse—and as we saw in Chapter 4, many humidifying arrangements are not at all complicated.

Also, most of the devices that control the operation of greenhouse systems are not technologically complex. Usually they are simply variations on the type of thermostats we use in our homes, since it is heat (or the absence of it) that causes the need for activation of these systems. The exceptions would be the humidistat, also a relatively

A thermometer is most accurate when it is shaded from the heat, as with this simple cowl. A thermostat, too, should be shaded. This mechanically operated jalousie door will prevent buildup of heat and poor air circulation in greenhouse. These units can be thermostatically controlled. Here is a closeup of a thermostat controlling an automatic venting device. Note protection from direct sun. (Courtesy Lord & Burnham)

An automatic thermostat

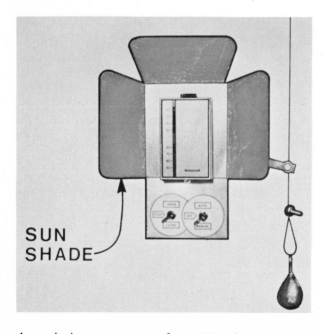

A sun shade—to prevent sun from raising thermostat temperature.

simple unit, and the clock timers, similar to the units used to turn house lights on at intervals when the occupants are away. Ordinary thermometers, of course, also play an important part in the greenhouse.

None of these devices, nor the appliances they control in the sizes required for home greenhouse use, is prohibitively expensive. Self-contained coolers, for example, are available for less than $200, while an automatic ventilator might cost half that amount. Compared to the investment in both money and effort represented by a healthy collection of plants, they are cheap insurance indeed.

Automation, to some degree, is doubtless a boon to the greenhouse owner, but there are limitations to the capabilities of even the most elaborate systems. This is the way it should be, as we mentioned in the opening chapter; otherwise, the gardener might as well turn to a different hobby. Machines cannot isolate plants suspected of disease; nor can they take the necessary precautions to see that insects and diseases do not get a foothold in the greenhouse. Machines cannot fuss over seedlings, or decide when cuttings should be taken from mature plants, or when to prune back a stalky or gangly specimen. These are the prerogatives of the gardener.

ARTIFICIAL LIGHTING

Before leaving the subject of electrical aids in the greenhouse, let's take up the question of lighting. Ordinarily the need for artificial light will not extend beyond an incandescent bulb or two enabling work to be done at night. But in special circumstances, growers may want to help plants along with lights so placed as to prolong daytime conditions. This will be especially easy to accomplish in the leanto, with its ready access to electricity.

When are growing lights desirable? There are those who have no choice but to build a north-facing greenhouse; although heating costs will remain high, the best may be made of such a situation by installing fluorescent lights. These will encourage flowering plants, which are often inhibited by the insufficient natural lighting offered by a northern exposure.

Fluorescents are most frequently installed along the eaves of a greenhouse; however, they may be arranged along the wall beneath benches, in order to convert unused space into a growing area. It is important that lights so installed not come into contact with water.

Artificial lighting can also be used to offset the effects of prolonged bad weather; in proper amounts during the winter, it can reverse some plants' tendencies

Flowering plants, like this exotic Bird-of-Paradise, like plenty of natural light.

Hold the light meter at arm's length in an open fully-exposed area of the greenhouse.

towards dormancy at that time of year. There is a long list of plants preferring long days; these will not normally thrive even in summer in northern latitudes, but can be made to flourish given the proper amount of extra artificial light at day's end.

Fluorescent lighting, which produces less heat, is preferable to incandescent for growing purposes. Likewise, particular types of fluorescents are recommended. If you cannot find bulbs made especially for indoor plants, select a "warm-white" variety, which produces a more favorable light.

An even simpler way to make fluorescents a part of your greenhouse is to buy a self-contained fixture. These units plug into a regular wall socket and may thus be installed anywhere within an extension cord's reach. They are often suspended from chains hung from eye hooks; the hooks are fastened into a shelf protruding over a plant bench, or sometimes to the underside of a bench itself. This latter arrangement converts dark, below-bench space to an area usable for small plants amenable to fluorescent light.

One reliable means of determining light intensity inside a greenhouse, and of deciding whether it should be increased, is to use a lightmeter. Gardeners familiar with photography will know how to read one of these.

Even for those who are not photographically inclined, the use of a lightmeter is not that difficult. You will not need to be concerned with f-stops, shutter speed, or any such functions that are associated only with the use of a camera. Simply set the "asa" indicator to a moderately "fast" position—200 should do—and concentrate on the reading that appears in the window at the top of the meter when it is held, unobstructed, in the natural light of the greenhouse. These numbers are exposure values to the photographer, but to the gardener they will be a simple indication of the available light in his enclosure. Readings consistently low on the scale show a lack of available sunlight—but don't be misled by a reading taken on a gloomy day. Take the lightmeter into the greenhouse over a succession of days, incorporating a wide range of weather conditions. A good sign of overall dimness will be the meter's inability to give a reading on its upper scale, which will come into view only when a hinged baffle is in place over the meter's "eye." If this baffle must be repeatedly folded out of the way, allowing the lower scale to appear in the window, chances are that overall light intensity in the greenhouse is poor. Some photo shops will rent meters.

FIXTURES AND MAINTENANCE

Climate control, watering, and lighting all benefit plants. Now it's time to consider some greenhouse amenities

FLUORESCENT LIGHT INSTALLATION

Fluorescent lighting may be easily installed above growing or work areas in the home greenhouse if a fixture box is conveniently located. When you are having your leanto or free-standing greenhouse wired, or if you are undertaking the job yourself, plan ahead. You should have a rough idea of where you will want the fixtures; the box should be placed accordingly. Even if you do not initially expect to install auxiliary lighting, a pre-installed box with available wiring connections will make an eventual lighting hookup much easier.

If a box is intended for immediate or eventual use with a fluorescent fixture, select a box with a threaded center stud, since most fluorescent housings are designed to be affixed to the box by means of a locknut fastened over this stud.

Installation is simple. After following the manufacturer's instructions for the assembly of the fluorescent fixture, position it over the box and pull the connecting wires through. Splice and cap the wires (white-to-white, black-to-black), and secure the fixture onto the box stud. Switching, if not remotely controlled by previous breaking of current flowing to the box, will be self-contained in the fluorescent unit by means of a button or chain.

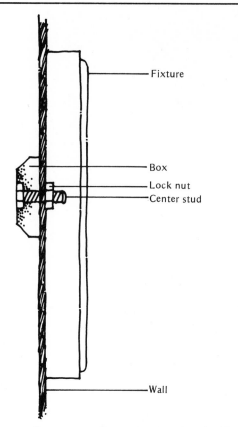

Fluorescent fixtures usually connect to electrical boxes by means of a lock nut fitting over a center stud in the box.

Here are two ways in which suspended, self-contained fluorescent fixtures can be mounted.

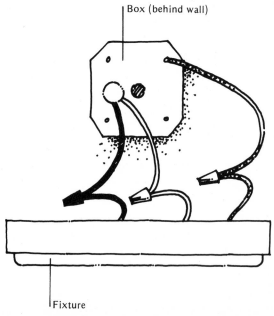

When installing fluorescents or any other light fixture, connect white to white and black to black wires—and be sure the current is shut off.

Here is another view of the sliding sink, showing hose hookup and shelf above.

This small sink, mounted on a sliding track, is a valuable space-saver in a leanto greenhouse.

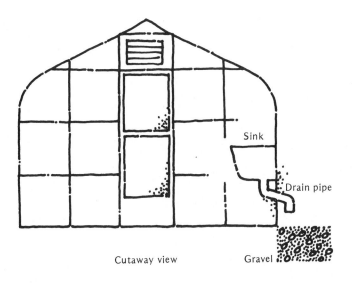

Cutaway view Gravel

Sink

Drain pipe

The greenhouse sink can be installed to drain into an outside gravel bed.

designed to benefit the man or woman who works with them. The layout of benches, walkways—of the greenhouse itself—can make a big difference in efficiency and convenience. So can the arrangement of the facilities used in day-to-day work in the indoor garden.

The greenhouse sink

One of the first such facilities you'll want is a sink—if not a conventional, running-water model, at least a basin served by a hose and with some provision for drainage. A sink will be useful for scrubbing pots, washing tools and hands, and perhaps even as the main connection point for the greenhouse watering hose.

Drainage may take the form of a hose or plastic pipe leading to a gravel-bed drain below the foundation, if the floor is of brick or concrete, or directly outside into loose stone or gravel if mud would be a problem indoors. (Remember that these types of drains—and even those emptying into a septic tank or town sewage system—are no place to dispose of pesticides that could find their way into the water table.)

The sink or basin will probably be located in an adjacent shed or a utility corner in a large greenhouse, but there are ways to make it as unobtrusive as possible in a small area where space is at a premium. One Vermont leanto owner has designed a sliding apparatus with which he can tuck his basin under a plant bench. When it is pulled into position, his utility hose is clamped into place as a makeshift faucet. A more permanent fixture could be installed in a leanto using an extension line to a pre-existing foundation spigot.

A work area

Only owners of the smallest, easiest-to-maintain freestanding greenhouses will want to carry their tools, pots,

Picture of shelves in greenhouse.

Don't overlook below-bench areas as valuable storage space. These miniature plastic trash barrels are ideal for storing potting soil and fertilizer.

and other equipment from the house or garage on gardening days. Larger operations will require that a special on-site area be reserved for storage purposes, as well as for auxiliary gardening work. This area can be either a separate structure (consider an old backyard shed as the startoff point for an attached even-span) or a part of the greenhouse not used for planting. Properly planned and stocked, it can be the "command center" for the whole garden, both indoors and out.

The simplest work area can be an extension of the plant bench frame topped with plywood, masonite, or other flat lumber, rather than the high-sided trays used for pots or soil. If space permits, shelves may be mounted above; some greenhouse manufacturers sell shelf supports designed to attach onto the building frame. Shelves placed above plant benches are best made of glass, mesh, or perforated aluminum, as these will not interfere with sunlight.

The space beneath the bench can be used for storage of heavier items, such as hoses, large pots, and bags of soil, fertilizer, and potting compound. It would be ideal to cluster all maintenance-related implements in the same corner with the sink and perhaps the heater; if there is any part of the greenhouse that is warmer, cooler, or more drafty than your plants might like, then there's the spot for a work area. Get into the habit of keeping tools and supplies there, and the greenhouse will be more attractive to look at as well as being easier to work in.

We saw earlier that a leanto greenhouse can be built so that access is from the basement, rather than from the first floor. In this case the problem of a work and storage area is solved; the small size of the growing area can be compensated for by the extra space available on the other side of the entry (in the cellar).

Tools and supplies

The particular implements necessary for cultivation of greenhouse plants will already be known to outdoor gardeners and houseplant enthusiasts and need not be described. It is worth noting, though, that in nearly all home greenhouse ventures the hobbyist will benefit from choosing light, compact versions of the familiar tools. These will be less cumbersome to work with in close quarters and can be stored conveniently on pegboards or shelves in the work area. Loose materials such as sand, soil, vermiculite, and fertilizer are best stored in tight-lidded plastic trash containers or, for smaller quantities, kitchen canisters. Select containers that will fit neatly under benches, or on shelves.

The proper storage of pesticides, fungicides, and other poisons is a matter of utmost concern for all gardeners, both indoors and out. Always keep these substances in clearly labeled, tightly closed containers, and if the greenhouse itself cannot be locked, store them in a locked chest in your work area or potting shed. They should never be left where children or animals can get at them, or where they can find their way into water or soil in which they are not meant to be used.

UPKEEP: SOME GENERAL IDEAS AND A CHECKLIST

As with everything from automobiles to teeth, the maintenance routine in a greenhouse becomes easier the more regularly it is followed. Day-to-day chores will pile up into monumental tasks by summer, if they are not taken care of as they arise.

The cleaning of pots is one example. All clay pots (and clay is the best kind) become encrusted, with use, with a brittle compound of algae and chemical salts. To be ready for the next planting, each pot should be scrubbed clean of this encrustation with a wire brush. Taken two or three at a time, this is not a difficult or unpleasant task—but if it is ignored, there will come a day when perhaps 50 or 100 pots all need scrubbing, and none are available for the potting work at hand.

What is true of the frequent care of planting equipment is likewise true of the maintenance of the greenhouse and its fixtures. Here the schedule will call for careful attention perhaps once or twice a year; but it is this thorough inspection and touch-up work that will prevent major trouble later on.

A checklist of annual or bi-annual maintenance procedures might include the following items:

- Remove all weeds, roots, too, from corners and under benches of dirt-floored greenhouses.

- Scrub frames of wooden greenhouses to remove fungi; repaint or treat with preservative when necessary.

- Check steel parts for rust; brush and paint where needed.

- Touch up paint-on shading, if used; check rolling shades for smooth operation.

- Once a year, on a warm, pleasant day (not a scorcher), move plants outdoors and wash down inside glass or fiberglass surfaces. Check plastic film for damage; replace or repair where needed. Repair cracked putty around glazing.

- While plants are outdoors, check for insects or slugs and spray before bringing them back inside. This is especially important where plants have been outdoors throughout the warm season.

- Gather together stray pots, tools, fertilizer bags, etc.; throw out what is not needed, and store the rest conveniently.

- Inspect all climate-control devices: heaters, coolers, fans, vents, etc. Check accuracy of timing and thermostatic devices. Warm weather is the time when your heating man should take care of routine service on oil and gas burners.

Keep pesticides and other poisonous substances under lock and key—and out of reach of children.

Keep a good supply of clean pots on hand—clean them a few at a time, on a regular basis.

These few operations, most of which can be performed in a day, will assure many more days of pleasure and relaxation in the new home greenhouse.

Light transmission is adversely affected by soiled glass lights. An occasional hosing and drying with squeegee will keep them clean.

Chapter 6 SOILS AND PLANTING

The last phase in setting up the new home greenhouse will be to ready it for "moving-in day." The principal chore involved here is the selection of the proper growing medium for plants in the greenhouse environment—pots, flats and trays, and above all, soils.

POTS

A flowerpot might seem the simplest thing in the world; but as anyone knows who has had even a modest amount of experience with houseplants, there are a variety of pot types and several important rules pertaining to their use.

The best-known pot, and to many gardeners simply the best, is the familiar one made of clay. Its advantages lie in its porousness—it can "breathe," as well as allow excess water to evaporate through its sides. These are available in literally dozens of sizes, for every conceivable indoor gardening purpose.

Pots of light plastic have begun to appear over the past few years. While they lack the porousness of clay, they are far less fragile and much lighter. Although they are built with drainage holes in the bottom, they will require the greenhouse gardener to be extremely cautious about overwatering. Also, the moisture released into the air through the evaporation of water from the walls of clay pots can be a beneficial humidifying factor—and will not occur with plastic pots.

A third pot variety is made of pressed peat. These are designed for the potting of young plants that are

As assortment of the pots commonly used in greenhouse gardening.

eventually destined for either larger pots or the outdoors. As the plant grows, the roots will poke through the peat. Then it is time to transplant, degradable pot and all.

Certain guidelines—such as the need for good drainage—apply to potting in all types of containers. This problem is usually solved by placing a shallow layer of

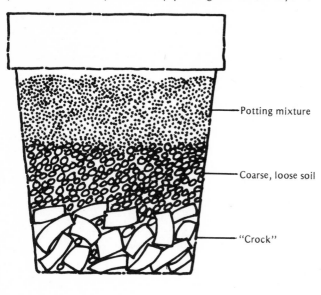

Cutaway view

The plant's actual growing medium should be tamped in over a bottom layer of broken pottery, or "crock," and a middle layer of coarse soil.

coarse gravel or broken clay pottery—called "crock"— in the bottom of each pot. The next layer of soil is coarse and loose, with the actual potting mixture forming the final layer.

Just as the above precautions are necessary to ensure that roots do not lie saturated in water that has no place to go, there are others that prevent too-quick drying of the soil and root system. To avoid this, always soak clay pots in water before using. Wait until they are completely saturated. Otherwise, the porous clay will draw water away from the soil and roots. This is also necessary with peat pots, although the soaking need not be as prolonged—these useful but delicate pots will disintegrate if they are left to soak for too long.

Pots vs. flats

In the greenhouse, flats and trays will be employed as well as individual pots. Their use will probably be confined to the propagation of seedlings and the growing of beds of compact vegetable crops such as lettuce or radishes. This is because the larger and more mature plants are more likely to need treatment as individuals, with differing soil and water requirements. You will also want to be able to "quarantine" a specimen suspected of disease or insect infestation, both of which are less easily communicated when plants are isolated in separate pots.

The requirements for drainage, however, remain the same whether plants are growing in pots or flats. In

The combination of compartmentalized trays and a sunny, temperature-controlled greenhouse environment is an ideal one for starting seedlings.

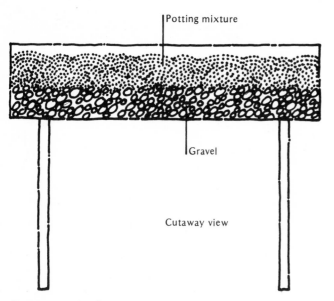

Drainage in the flat is similar to that in pots, with coarse gravel forming the bottom layer.

an earlier chapter we saw that benches are best constructed with a provision for drainage. Building them with high-walled trays that can accommodate either pots or loose soil will prevent water accumulation. (An exception would be when troughed benches are lined with plastic in order to hold a water-soaked medium, intended to transmit moisture to clay pots while the gardener is away.) The technique for ensuring adequate drainage in soil-filled flats is the same as that used when potting plants: use a coarse gravel base before applying the growing medium itself. Remember that flats are most frequently used for germination, and that young seedlings are especially vulnerable to excessive moisture.

SOIL: MORE THAN JUST DIRT

It is when we come to the subject of soil itself that the novice gardener is most likely to become confused. Those with previous experience, indoor and out, will

This is the proper texture for potting soil—compressible, yet easily crumbled.

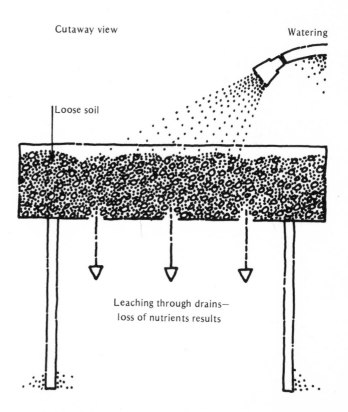

The leaching process can rob greenhouse soil of valuable nutrients.

Although pre-sterilized soils are available, the gardener can save money by "baking" soil in a kitchen oven to remove danger of pests.

Vermiculite, shown here being added to a potting tray, lightens the soil, preventing it from compacting around roots.

know that soil is not simply soil: the best potting medium for greenhouse plants—as well as for any others—is a careful composition of the right textures and nutrients. The most desirable soil texture for potting greenhouse plants is best described in the word "friable," which means that the soil is just moist and compact enough to form a solid mass when pressure is applied, but will crumble readily thereafter. This quality is not so easily found in "clayey" soils, which are dense to the point of inhibiting root growth in pots and flats. Soils too loose, however, will allow water to pass through too quickly and "leach" out nutrients through drainage.

The texture of soil is the result of its composition. Gardeners are familiar with the varieties of earth that go to make up good garden soil: sand, which breaks up the density of tightly packed soils and facilitates drainage; humus, the rich residue of decayed organic matter; clay, which must be balanced with lighter elements but which

is needed for its mineral content; and the nutrient-rich peats and manure. The name given to soils that incorporate a variety of these "building blocks" is *loam.* This is the soil that will be found in the outdoor garden.

Add to these naturally occurring soils the synthetic substances such as perlite and vermiculite, and it will be possible—with fertilization, where needed—to create the proper growing medium for just about any greenhouse plants. The two above-mentioned synthetics are useful not only for lightening and aerating potting mixtures, but for using unmixed as a rooting medium for new cuttings. They have the advantage of being entirely free of disease and harmful bacteria; this is an advantage that can also be enjoyed with commercial potting soils and home-sterilized mixtures.

Sterilization

Sterilizing soil at home need not be complicated or elaborate. There are machines—timed, temperature-controlled electric ovens, really—that are designed for the heat-sterilization of greenhouse and garden soils; these are impractical unless a good deal of soil is to be sterilized regularly. The home greenhouse enthusiast is not likely to be able to justify their expense. Sterilization can therefore also be accomplished in the kitchen oven, even though warm soil has a rather distinctive smell. Use a slow setting (about 175 degrees) and bake in moderate quantities in an old roasting pan for about 40 or 50 minutes. This will kill nematodes, harmful insect larvae, and weed roots and seeds. Don't leave the soil in the oven too long, or at too high a temperature, because it is possible to "burn" the earth and neutralize important nutrients.

An alternative to home-sterilizing soil is to buy package soil from nurserymen, garden supply houses, or florists. This product may then be mixed, if desired, with other clean soil components in order to attain the texture and nutrient composition needed in the greenhouse.

The soil test kit is easy to use, and will provide a quick and easy analysis of your soil's nutritional makeup.

Soil nutrients and "pH"

Even if you have selected your plant stocks to fit a certain temperature and humidity range, it is probable that they will differ in their potting requirements. This, of course, is why individual pots are preferable to mass plantings in soil-filled beds. The gardener coming to terms with these diverse requirements will have to face the question of soil nutrients as well as that of texture. Here is where soil testing, fertilizers, and the pH factor come into play.

If you are uncertain as to the nutritional quality of the soil you are bringing into the greenhouse—if, for instance, you have not already been using it for an outdoor garden or are going to be growing plants of an entirely different variety indoors—it is a good idea to test the soil. This is not difficult; most garden shops sell kits that enable the amateur to run the test himself. If you prefer, most state agricultural colleges or Extension Services will test it for you, if you send them a representative soil sample in a plastic bag.

The idea behind a soil test is to turn up evidence of possible mineral insufficiencies, and to determine the overall relationship between acidity and alkalinity in the soil. This is where the shorthand symbol "pH" comes in; its number value merely signifies the acid-alkaline ratio. It is simple to understand: 7.0 indicates an even balance; smaller numbers show higher acidity, and numbers above 7.0 indicate an essentially alkaline soil. From here it is a matter of judiciously applying the right fertilizing agent in order to bring the pH to the level required by your plants. It is helpful, in a large greenhouse where plants of differing requirements grow, to keep on hand a supply of potting soils reflecting the various preferences of your plants.

STOCKING THE PLANTS

The soil has been stocked; a steady source of it (perhaps no farther away than your own garden) has been found. Beds and pots are to be filled according to the texture and nutritional requirements of each plant species—and a

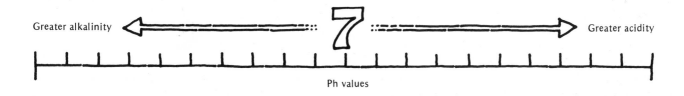

Greater alkalinity ⟵ - - - - - - - - - - - - - - 7 - - - - - - - - - - - - - ⟶ Greater acidity

Ph values

Seven is the median on the Ph value scale.

good supply of pots is on hand to serve the plants as they proceed through their stages of growth. It remains only for you to bring in the plants; then your greenhouse will be complete. No doubt some will come from inside your home, and it is equally likely that you will be given plants as "greenhousewarming" presents. You'll know the condition of your houseplants, but with gifts and other new acquisitions it will be necessary to segregate them from beds of new seedlings and established healthy plants until they have shown themselves free of diseases and/or insects. Greenhouse quarters are close; an attack of mealy bugs or fungus can spread quickly and devastatingly.

It is also important to find a reliable source for greenhouse stock—perhaps the same supplier you have depended on for outdoor gardening needs. In time, you will have a burgeoning population of young plants yourself, and potted, mature specimens from your greenhouse will begin to spread among your friends and circle of garden enthusiasts. The satisfaction of such successful ventures, as well as the enjoyment you derive from hours of work in an atmosphere of color, quiet, and tranquility, are the best rewards of the home greenhouse.

There are always ways to keep busy in the greenhouse. This gardener wears a protective mask as he sprays insecticide from a portable atomizer unit.

A GREENHOUSE GLOSSARY

A-frame Type of greenhouse distinguished by walls sloping directly from ground to ridge of roof, giving an overall triangular or "A" shape.

Ambient temperature Average temperature maintained for growing plants in greenhouse.

Battens Light wooden strips used for holding plastic film down evenly while applying; also similar strips installed permanently over studs to which film is nailed.

Breaker nozzle Attachment for end of hose to break force of water spray.

British thermal units A measurement used to determine the capacity of heating systems. One BTU is the amount of energy required to heat one pound of water one degree Fahrenheit, at a temperature of 39.2 degrees.

Bulb pan A wide-mouthed, shallow clay or other pot designed to accommodate bulb plants.

Clay A dense, mineral-rich soil variety (adjective: clayey).

Coldframe A flat, glass-topped bed heated only by the sun. Used for early stages of growth and "hardening-off" of plants before weather allows them to be planted outside.

Conservatory Term often used interchangeably with "greenhouse;" more properly refers to a glass enclosure meant only for display of ornamental plants.

Convection tube Ventilation device in which air is distributed into the greenhouse through openings in a plastic duct suspended from the ceiling.

Crock Broken pottery; usually shards of old clay pots. Used to facilitate drainage at bottom of pots.

Damping-down Process of wetting gravel and masonry surfaces inside greenhouse to increase humidity.

Damping-off Disorder of germinating seedlings, in which plants are killed by an excess of moisture.

Dibble stick A pointed stick (pencils can be used) with which holes are made in seedflat soil to receive seeds. A board to which uniform rows of these sticks are attached is called a "dibble board."

Dome See Geodesic dome.

Double-thick Grade of glass usually recommended for greenhouse glazing; it generally weighs about 24 ounces per square foot.

Drainage In greenhouses, refers to measures taken to prevent muddy floors and boggy surroundings; in potting, refers to adequate provision for water runoff at bottom of pot.

Dutch-type Greenhouse design characterized by a "gambrel" roof, with walls splayed outwards.

Eaves Area of greenhouse at which walls intersect roof.

Even-span Symmetrical greenhouse design in which distance from ground to ridge of roof is equal at both ends.

Exposure The direction toward which the glass wall of an attached greenhouse faces, as in an eastern or western exposure.

Flats Shallow boxes used for propagation of seedlings.

Free-standing A greenhouse unattached to any larger structure.

Friable Desirable condition of soil; it can be compressed but still crumbles easily.

Frost-line   In northern climates, the deepest underground level at which frost can be expected to take hold. Important in calculating necessary foundation depth.

Fungus   (adjective: fungous) A family of plant diseases brought on by excessive moisture, as when leaves lie in water or overly saturated soil.

Gables   The triangular spaces formed at opposite ends of a symmetrical, even-span roof.

Geodesic dome   Design in which triangular panels form a domed structure; favored for its strength, lightness, and even distribution of stress.

Germination   The process of sprouting in seeds.

Glass-to-ground   Greenhouse design in which top of foundation wall is nearly flush with ground level, allowing glass to extend for full length of walls.

Glazing   The process by which glass or a substitute is applied to the greenhouse frame; also, the transparent portion of a greenhouse.

Gothic   Greenhouse design in which walls taper, arch-like, to a point at roof ridge.

Hardening-off   Process of acclimating plants to colder outdoor environment after propagation in greenhouse or hotbed; usually done in coldframe.

Hotbed   Shallow, glass-topped structure similar to coldframe, but heated with electric cables, steam pipes, or confined manure.

Humidistat   Device that reads level of humidity in greenhouse atmosphere and activates humidifier accordingly.

Humus   Rich soil composed largely of residue from decomposing organic matter.

Jalousie   Type of greenhouse window or vent in which diagonally placed panels are angled open, and closed, by means of a crank.

Kiln-dried   Term applied to lumber that has been dried in a kiln, as opposed to drying by simple exposure to air. Kiln-dried lumber is less likely to warp or shrink and is recommended for greenhouse construction.

Leaching   Process in which minerals or components of soil are carried downwards through water drainage. Can be an undesirable activity, or one done deliberately to remove certain excesses.

Leanto   Greenhouse sharing one of its longer sides with a larger structure.

Lights   In glass greenhouses, refers to individual window sections.

Louvres   (also: louvers) A series of diagonally installed vent panels used as an air intake in tandem with an exhaust fan.

Mil   Unit of measurement equal to one-thousandth of an inch. Used in measuring thickness of plastic films used to cover greenhouse frames.

Misting   The process of introducing an aerated stream of fast-evaporating water into the greenhouse environment.

Misting nozzle   Attachment used at end of hose to create fine mist.

Nematodes   Threadlike, nearly invisible soil pests which can do great harm to plant roots. They can be eliminated by sterilizing potting soil.

Ornamentals   Those plants which are raised for their esthetic value alone.

Peat   A valuable nutrient and soil lightener composed of the remains of long-dead vegetation. Not to be used as a bed for soil-heating cables.

Perlite   A light, artificial rooting medium useful for potting new cuttings and lightening soil.

pH   Represents the balance of acidity and alkalinity; using numerical value as symbol, 7.0 equals perfect balance.

Pitch   Degree of steepness of greenhouse roof.

Quonset   Greenhouse design resembling half of a horizontal cylinder; generally built with fiberglass covering.

Ridge   The highest point of the greenhouse roof.

Rootbound   Condition in which roots of plant have outgrown a pot, and are bound together and turned inwards.

Rose   Bulbous, perforated attachment at the end of a watering-can spout; breaks stream of water.

Sand   In potting, refers not to beach sand but to the clean, sharp sand used by masons.

Sash   The movable, glass-paned parts of windows. Sashes are sometimes used for glazing hotbeds and coldframes.

Seedlings   State of growth of plants in days immediately following germination.

Single-thick   Lighter glass, usually 16 ounces per square foot, not recommended for glazing greenhouses.

Sterilization   (Sometimes called pasteurization). Process in which soil is heated to a certain temperature in order to kill undesirable insects and bacteria.

Thermostat   Heat-sensitive device used to activate greenhouse heating and cooling systems.

Translucent Not completely transparent; partially light-inhibiting.

Turbolator Trade name for an air-circulating device with bread-mixer-like blades.

Vermiculite Synthetic potting mixture composed chiefly of ground mica. May be used to lighten soil.

Volume In calculating heating and ventilation requirements, refers to total volume (length X width X height) of greenhouse.

Whitewash Lime-based substance sometimes applied as shading to greenhouse lights. Do not use near aluminum.

Zone In heating, a system of pipes or ducts serving a subarea of the heated structure. Zones may be added to installations of sufficient capacity.

Appendix A   STOCKING THE WINTER GREENHOUSE

The accompanying chart shows a northern greenhouse as it might be stocked in winter. This greenhouse may be assumed to lie in the southern lee of a house or other larger building, giving it protection from harsh winds; the longer sides face east and west. The larger section to the right is heated to a nighttime temperature of 55–60 degrees Fahrenheit; the smaller, partitioned-off section is kept at a 50-degree maximum. Remember that morning sunlight, which comes from the east, is most beneficial to flowering plants. The western exposure may be shaded from this strong morning light by the use of blinds on the ridge-to-eave section of the eastern exposure. The northern end of this structure will receive the least amount of light.

The numbered listings below correspond to the numbers shown in the plant bench section of the diagram.

1. *Pilea cadieri* (Aluminum Plant)

2. *Caladium*

3. *Adiantum tenerum* (Maidenhair Fern)—(Keep from direct sun)

4. Coleus

5. Bromeliads

6. Poinsettia (Keep from direct light—perhaps under bench—until established)

7. *Impatiens* (Touch-me-not)

8. *Polianthes tuberosa* (Tuberose)

9. Gladiolus

10. Iris

11. *Hippeastrum* (Amaryllis)

12. *Asparagus plumosus* (Asparagus Fern)

13. *Aucuba japonica v.* (Gold-Dust Tree)

14. *Pittosporum tobira* (Japanese Pittosporum)

15. Camellia

16. *Chlorophytum* (Spider Plant)—(Hanging)

17. *Osmanthus fragrans* (Sweet Olive)—(Against warm wall)

18. *Primula* (Primrose)

19. *Hedera helix* (English Ivy)

20. Fuchsia—(Hanging)

21. Cyclamen—(Shade at midday)

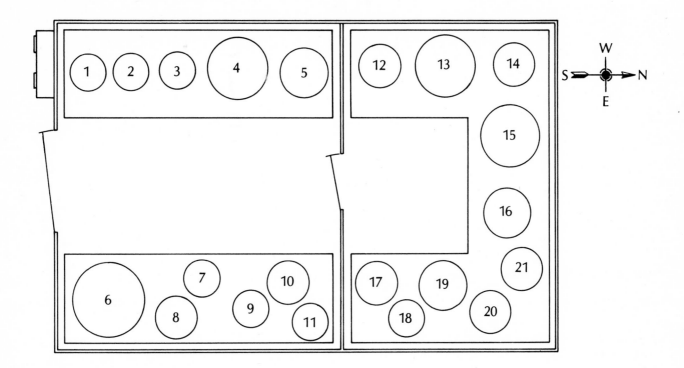

Appendix B PLANTS FOR NORTHERN CLIMATES

The plants listed in the following table are especially suited for cultivation in the cool northern greenhouse; all of them do well given a night temperature of 45–55 degrees Fahrenheit. They are by no means the only plants suited for northern climates; however, their requirements offer a good opportunity for beginning greenhouse enthusiasts in northern climates to diversify their planting without excessive application of artificial heat.

Name	Lighting	Water	Soil (unless normal mix)	Other Comments
Acacia	Full sun	Keep moist	Sandy loam	Very cool nights preferred
Anemone coronaria (Windflower)	Moderate shade	Average		Blooms only if kept at 45-50 degrees during night
Aucuba japonica v. (Gold Dust Tree)	Moderate shade	Keep dry		Fresh air important
Beleropone guttata (Shrimp Plant)	Full sun	Dry between soakings		Fresh air important
Calceolaria crenatiflora (Lady's Pocketbook)	Moderate shade	Water carefully		Prefers extra light in evening
Calendula officinalis (Pot Marigold)	Full sun	Water freely		
Camellia	Moderate shade	Plenty		Require little care. Grow quite tall.
Campanula isophylla (Bellflower)	Full sun	Water well; let dry in between		
Chrysanthemums	Moderate shade	Keep soil moist; mist		Grow tall; need supports
Cyclamen	Moderate shade	Keep moist	Fresh loam; 1/5 manure	Sensitive to many pesticides
Dianthus Caryophyllus (Carnation)	Moderate shade	Moderate	Sand (for rooting cuttings)	Good ventilation important
Eschscholzia california (California Poppy)	Moderate shade	Moderate		Do not allow to crowd

Ferns	Moderate shade	Keep moist		Avoid drafts
Fuchsia	Full sun	Keep moist		Good air circulation necessary
Gypsophila	Moderate shade	Moderate		
Hedera helix (English Ivy)	Full sun	Moist; not soggy		Good air circulation necessary
Lathyrus odoratus (Sweet-Pea)	Moderate shade	Water well when sunny	Rich, clayey soil; good drainage	Do not crowd
Lobularia maritima (Sweet-Alyssum)	Moderate shade	Moderate		
Myosotis sylvatica (Forget-Me-Not)	Moderate shade	Plenty		
Nerine sarniensis (Guernsey-Lily)	Moderate shade	Dry at first; moist while growing		Good drainage important
Primula (Primrose)	Full sun	Water well	High humus content	
Saxifraga sarmentosa (Strawberry Begonia)	Moderate sun	Water well; let dry in between		
Trachelospermum jasminoides (Star-Jasmine)	Moderate sun	Moderate		
Tritonia crocosmaeflora	Full sun	Moist; not wet		
Tropaeolum majus (Nasturtium)	Full sun	Moderate	Grows well in poor soil	
Tulbaghia cepacea	Full sun	Moderate to moist		
Veltheimia viridiflora	Moderate shade	Water thoroughly while flowering	Rich, fibrous soil with charcoal and sand	

Below is a list of plants, representing both flowering and foliage varieties, commonly grown in homes and greenhouses. They are listed according to their preference for cool, medium or warm greenhouse environment.

Plant	Temperature*		
	Warm	Medium	Cool
Acorus			x
African Violet			x
Aloe			x
Amaryllis		x	
Anthurium	x		
Asparagus Fern		x	
Avocado		x	
Begonia		x	
Bird of Paradise			x
Bougainvillea		x	
Caladium	x		
Calla Lily		x	
Camellia			x
Christmas Cactus		x	
Clematis		x	
Clivia		x	
Coleus	x		
Columnea		x	
Creeping Fig		x	
Dieffenbachia		x	
Dracaena		x	
Fittonia	x		
Flame Violet	x		
Fuschia			x
Gardenia		x	
Gloxinia		x	
Hibiscus		x	
Hoya			x

Plant	Temperature*		
	Warm	Medium	Cool
Hydrangea			x
Impatiens			x
Ivy, English			x
Ivy, Swedish			x
Ivy, Geranium			x
Jade Plant			x
Maidenhair Fern		x	
Miniature Rose		x	
Myrtle			x
Oleander		x	
Orchid (Tiger)		x	
Peperomia		x	
Philodendron (split leaf)			x
Pilea (aluminum)		x	
Purple Passion, Velvet Plant	x		
Rhodendron			x
Sansevieria	x		
Saxifraga			x
Scindapsus	x		
Screw Pine		x	
Sensitive Plant		x	
Spider Plant			x
Stephanotis		x	
Sweet-Olive			x
Tolmeia (Piggyback)			x
Walking Iris			x
Wandering Jew			x
Zebra Plant		x	

*Greenhouse nighttime temperatures—Cool: mid-40's, medium: Mid-50's, warm: 60 or over.

Appendix C COOPERATIVE EXTENSION SERVICE DIRECTORS

The Cooperative Extension Service, a joint effort of the United States Department of Agriculture and the colleges of agriculture in each state, maintains home offices at main campuses in the states as well as county offices, each staffed by agents trained in agriculture and home economics. Among the personnel at Extension headquarters in each state are agricultural engineers, who are able to assist in matters pertaining to the construction and maintenance of greenhouses, and botanists and gardening specialists, who can help the home horticulturist in raising both vegetables and ornamentals. Extension publication offices are also the source of many helpful government brochures on gardening.

The following is a list of the directors of state Extension Services. Questions addressed to them will be referred to the proper specialists. Greenhouse gardeners should also become familiar with the location and staff of their county Extension offices.

Alabama

W. H. Taylor, Auburn University,
Auburn, Alabama 36830

Alaska

J. W. Matthews, University of Alaska,
College, Alaska 99701

Arizona

G. R. Stairs, Acting Director,
University of Arizona, Tucson, Arizona 85721

Arkansas

Ken Bates, Box 391, Little Rock,
Arkansas, 72203

California

G. B. Alcorn, University of California,
2200 University Avenue, Berkeley,
California 94720

Colorado

L. H. Watts, Colorado State University,
Fort Collins, Colorado 80521

Connecticut

E. J. Kersting, University of Connecticut,
Storrs, Connecticut 06268

District of Columbia

John Jenkins, Acting Director,
Federal City College, 1424 K Street NW,
Washington, D.C. 20005

Delaware

S. M. Gwinn, University of Delaware,
Newark, Delaware 19711

Florida

J. N. Busby, University of Florida,
Gainesville, Florida 32601

Georgia

Charles P. Ellington, University of Georgia,
Athens, Georgia 30601

Hawaii

D. N. Goodell, Acting Director,
University of Hawaii, Honolulu,
Hawaii 96822

Idaho

James L. Graves, University of Idaho,
Moscow, Idaho 83843

Illinois

J. B. Claar, University of Illinois,
Urbana, Illinois 61801

Indiana

H. G. Diesslin, Purdue University,
Lafayette, Indiana 47907

Iowa

M. A. Anderson, Iowa State University,
Ames, Iowa 50010

Kansas

R. A. Bohannon, Kansas State University,
Manhattan, Kansas 66502

Kentucky

C. E. Barnhart, University of Kentucky,
Lexington, Kentucky 40506

Louisiana

J. A. Cox, Louisiana State University,
Baton Rouge, Louisiana 70803

Maine

E. H. Bates, University of Maine,
Orono, Maine 04473

Maryland

R. E. Wagner, University of Maryland,
College Park, Maryland 20742

Massachusetts

A. A. Spielman, University of Massachusetts,
Amherst, Massachusetts 01002

Michigan

Gordon Guyer, Michigan State University,
East Lansing, Michigan 48823

Minnesota

R. H. Abraham, University of Minnesota,
St. Paul, Minnesota 55101

Mississippi

W. M. Bost, Mississippi State University,
Mississippi 39762

Missouri

Carl N. Scheneman, University of Missouri,
Columbia, Missouri 65201

Montana

R. F. Bucher, Montana State University,
Bozeman, Montana 59715

Nebraska

J. L. Adams, University of Nebraska,
Lincoln, Nebraska 68503

Nevada

D. W. Bohmont, University of Nevada,
Reno, Nevada 89507

New Hampshire

Maynard C. Heckel, University of
New Hampshire, Durham,
New Hampshire 03824

New Jersey

J. L. Gerwig, Rutgers University,
New Brunswick, New Jersey 08903

New Mexico

P. J. Leyendecker, New Mexico State University,
Las Cruces, New Mexico 88001

New York

David L. Call, New York State
College of Agriculture,
Ithaca, New York 14850

North Carolina

G. Hyatt, Jr., North Carolina
State University,
Raleigh, North Carolina 27607

North Dakota

M. D. Johnsrud, North Dakota State
University, Fargo, North Dakota 51802

Ohio

R. M. Kottman, Ohio State University,
2120 Fyffe Road, Columbus, Ohio 43210

Oklahoma

Frank Baker, Oklahoma State University,
Stillwater, Oklahoma 74074

Oregon

Joseph R. Cox, Oregon State University,
Corvallis, Oregon 97331

Pennsylvania

James M. Beattie, Pennsylvania State University,
University Park, Pennsylvania 16802

Rhode Island

Gerald A. Donovan, University of Rhode Island,
Kingston, Rhode Island 02881

South Carolina

W. T. O'Dell, Clemson University,
Clemson, South Carolina 29631

South Dakota

H. Hall, Acting Director, South Dakota
State University, Brookings, South Dakota 57006

Tennessee

William D. Bishop, University of Tennessee,
Box 1071, Knoxville, Tennessee 37901

Texas

J. E. Hutchinson, Texas A & M University,
College Station, Texas 77843

Utah

Clark Ballard, Utah State University,
Logan, Utah 84321

Vermont

R. P. Davison, University of Vermont,
Burlington, Vermont 05401

Virginia

W. E. Skelton, Virginia Polytechnic Institute,
Blacksburg, Virginia 24061

Washington

J. O. Young, Washington State University,
Pullman, Washington 99163

West Virginia

Ronald Stump, West Virginia University,
128 Wiley Street, Morgantown,
West Virginia 26506

Wisconsin

Gale L. VandeBerg, University of Wisconsin,

432 N. Lake Street,
Madison, Wisconsin 53706

Wyoming

Robert F. Frary, University of Wyoming,
Box 3354, University Station,
Laramie, Wyoming 82070

Canada

Agriculture Canada
Sir John Carling Bldg., Ottawa, Ont. K1A OC7
Attention: Dr. Carmari (Director), Mr. Ronayne
(Asst. Director), or Mrs. Sheila Davis (Executive
Assistant)

Mr. Richard Sparkes, Public Information
Dept. of Forestry and Agriculture
Confederation Building, St. John's, Nfld. A1C 5T7

Mr. Roger Younger, Information Officer
Extension Services, Dept. of Agriculture and Forestry
P.O. Box 2000, Charlottestown, P.E.I. C1A 7N8

Mr. Peter Stewart, Publications
Dept. of Agriculture and Marketing
Nova Scotia Agricultural College, Truto, N.S. B2N 5E3

Mrs. Deirde Grondin, Asst. Director
Dept. of Agriculture and Rural Development
Federicton, N.B. E3B 5H1

Mrs. Benoit Roy, Information Director
Dept. of Agriculture, Quebec, Que. C1A 1E4

Mrs. G. H. Ketemer, Associate Director
Information, Ministry of Agriculture and Food
Parliament Buildings, Toronto, Ont. M7A 1A5

Mr. Vern McNair, Communications, Dept. of Agriculture
307-200 Vaughan St., Winnipeg, Man. R3C 1T5

Mr. Roger C. Fry, Communications, Dept. of Agriculture
Administration Bldg., Regina, Sask. S4S 0B1

Mr. John R. Andrew, Communications, Alberta Agriculture
1V Agriculture Bldg., 9718-107th St.,
Edmonton, Alta. T5K 2C8

Mr. Ron Sera, Information, Dept. of Agriculture,
Parliament Bldgs., Victoria, B.C. V8W 2Z7

Appendix D SUPPLIERS OF GREENHOUSE KITS AND EQUIPMENT

Aluminum Greenhouses, Inc., 14615 Lorain Avenue, Cleveland, Ohio 44111

American Leisure Industries, Inc., P.O. Box 63, Deep River, Connecticut 06417

W. Atlee Burpee Company, Warminster, Pennsylvania 18974

Casa-Planta, 9489 Dayton Way, Suite 211, Beverly Hills, California 90210

Dome East, 325 Duffy Avenue, Hicksville, New York 11801

Geodesic Domes, R.R. 1, Bloomington, Illinois 61701

Ickes-Braun Greenhouse Manufacturing Co., Box 147, Deerfield, Illinois 60015

Lord and Burnham, Irvington, New York 14610 (also: Des Plaines, Illinois 60018)

National Greenhouse Company, Box 100, Pana, Illinois 62557

J. A. Nearing Co., Inc., 10788 Tucker Street, Beltsville, Maryland 20705

Redfern's Prefab Greenhouses, 55 Mt. Hermon Road, Scotts Valley, California 95060

Redwood Domes, 2664 Highway 1, Aptos, California 95003

Peter Reimuller, The Greenhouseman, P.O. Box 2666, Santa Cruz, California 95060

Sturdi-Built Manufacturing Company, 11304 S.W. Boones Ferry Road, Portland, Oregon 97219

Sun World Gardens, Inc., 10250 E. McDowell, Scottsdale, Arizona 85251

Texas Greenhouse Co., Inc., 2710 St. Louis Avenue, Fort Worth, Texas 76110

Turner Greenhouses, P.O. Box 1260, Goldsboro, North Carolina 27530

BIBLIOGRAPHY

Blake, Claire L. *Greenhouse Gardening for Fun.* New York: Barrows, 1967.

Crockett, James Underwood. *Greenhouse Gardening as a Hobby.* Garden City, N.Y.: Doubleday, 1961.

Dulles, Marion. *Greenhouse Gardening Around the Year.* New York: Macmillan, 1956.

Eaton, Jerome A. *Gardening Under Glass.* New York: Macmillan, 1973.

Lewis, C. C. *The Greenhouse.* New York: Pergamon Press, 1965.

McDonald, Elvin. *The Flowering Greenhouse Day by Day.* Princeton, N.J.: Van Nostrand, 1966.

Northern, H. T. and Northern, Rebecca T. *Greenhouse Gardening.* 2nd ed. New York: Ronald Press, 1973.

Potter, Charles H. *Beneath the Greenhouse Roof.* New York: Criterion Books, 1957.

Potter, Charles H. *Greenhouse: Place of Magic.* New York: E. P. Dutton, 1967.

The Wise Garden Encyclopedia. New York: Grosset and Dunlap, 1970.

INDEX

Other SUCCESSFUL Books

SUCCESSFUL SPACE SAVING AT HOME. The conquest of inner space in apartments, whether tiny or ample, and homes, inside and out. Storage and built-in possibilities for all living areas, with a special section of illustrated tips from the professional space planners. 8½″ x 11″; 128 pp; over 150 B-W and color photographs and illustrations. $12.00 Cloth. $4.95 Paper.

BOOK OF SUCCESSFUL HOME PLANS. Published in cooperation with Home Planners, Inc.; designs by Richard B. Pollman. A collection of 226 outstanding home plans, plus information on standards and clearances as outlined in HUD's *Manual of Acceptable Practices.* 8½″ x 11″; 192 pp; over 500 illustrations. $12.00 Cloth. $4.95 Paper.

FINDING & FIXING THE OLDER HOME, Schram. Tells how to check for tell-tale signs of damage when looking for homes and how to appraise and finance them. Points out the particular problems found in older homes, with instructions on how to remedy them. 8½″ x 11″; 160 pp; over 200 photographs and illustrations. $12.00 Cloth. $4.95 Paper.

WALL COVERINGS AND DECORATION, Banov. Describes and evaluates different types of papers, fabrics, foils and vinyls, and paneling. Chapters on art selection, principles of design and color. Complete installation instructions for all materials. 8½″ x 11″; 136 pp; over 150 B-W and color photographs and illustrations. $12.00 Cloth. $4.95 Paper.

BOOK OF SUCCESSFUL FIREPLACES, Lytle. How to build, decorate, and use all types of fireplaces. Covers fireplace construction, history, problems, cookery, even how to keep a good fire going. 8½″ x 11″; 104 pp; over 150 B-W and color photographs and illustrations. (Chosen by Popular Science Book Club). $12.00 Cloth. $4.95 Paper.

BOOK OF SUCCESSFUL KITCHENS, Galvin. In-depth information on building, decorating, modernizing, and using kitchens, by the editor of *Kitchen Business* magazine. 8½″ x 11″; 136 pp; over 200 B-W and color photographs and illustrations. $12.00 Cloth. $4.95 Paper.

BOOK OF SUCCESSFUL PAINTING, Banov. Everything about painting any surface, inside or outside. Includes surface preparation, paint selection and application, problems, and color in decorating. "Before dipping brush into paint, a few hours spent with this authoritative guide could head off disaster." —*Publishers Weekly.* 8½″ x 11″; 114 pp; over 150 B-W and color photographs and illustrations. $12.00 Cloth. $4.95 Paper.

BOOK OF SUCCESSFUL BATHROOMS, Schram. Complete guide to remodeling or decorating a bathroom to suit individual needs and tastes. Materials are recommended that have more than one function, need no periodic refinishing, and fit into different budgets. Complete installation instructions. 8½″ x 11″; 128 pp; over 200 B-W and color photographs. (Chosen by Interior Design, Woman's How-to, and Popular Science Book Clubs). $12.00 Cloth. $4.95 Paper.

TOTAL HOME PROTECTION, Miller. How to make your home burglarproof, fireproof, accidentproof, termiteproof, windproof, and lightningproof. With specific instructions and product recommendations. 8½″ x 11″; 124 pp; over 150 photographs and illustrations. (Chosen by McGraw-Hill's Architects Book Club). $12.00 Cloth. $4.95 Paper.

BOOK OF SUCCESSFUL SWIMMING POOLS, Derven and Nichols. Everything the present or would-be pool owner should know, from what kind of pool he can afford and site location, to construction, energy savings, accessories and maintenance and safety. 8½″ x 11″; 128 pp; over 250 B-W and color photographs and illustrations. $12.00 Cloth. $4.95 Paper.

HOW TO BUILD YOUR OWN HOME, Reschke. Construction methods and instructions for wood-frame ranch, one-and-a-half story, two-story, and split level homes, with specific recommendations for materials and products. 8½″ x 11″; 336 pp; over 600 photographs, illustrations, and charts. (Main selection for McGraw-Hill's Engineers Book Club). $14.00 Cloth. $5.95 Paper.

HOW TO CUT YOUR ENERGY BILLS, Derven and Nichols. A homeowner's guide designed not for just the fix-it person, but for everyone. Instructions on how to save money and fuel in all areas—lighting, appliances, insulation, caulking, and much more. If it's on your utility bill, you'll find it here. 8½″ x 11″; 136 pp; over 200 photographs and illustrations. $12.00 Cloth. $4.95 Paper.

Structures Publishing Company   Box 423   Farmington, Michigan 48024